BLOOD MEMORY

MARTHA GRAHAM

BLOOD MEMORY

DOUBLEDAY

NEW YORK LONDON TORONTO SYDNEY AUCKLAND

PUBLISHED BY DOUBLEDAY

a division of
Bantam Doubleday Dell Publishing Group, Inc.
666 Fifth Avenue, New York, New York 10103

DOUBLEDAY and the portrayal of an anchor
with a dolphin are trademarks of Doubleday,
a division of Bantam Doubleday Dell Publishing Group, Inc.

Excerpt from Wilderness Stair by Ben Belitt is reprinted by permission of the author, © 1955 by Ben Belitt.

Excerpts from Selected Poems and Letters by Emily Dickinson edited by Robert N. Linscott are reprinted by permission of Wendy T. Linscott, Executrix of the Estate of Robert N. Linscott, and Bantam Doubleday Dell Publishing Group, Inc.; © 1959 by Robert N. Linscott.

"Waltz Me Around Again Willie," words by Will D. Cobb, music by Ren Shields, copyright 1906 by F. A. Mills.

Frontispiece War Themes, 1941

Book design by Marysarah Quinn

Library of Congress Cataloging-in-Publication Data
Graham, Martha.
    Blood memory / Martha Graham.—1st ed.
        p. cm.
    1. Graham, Martha.   2. Choreographers—United States—Biography.
    3. Dancers—United States—Biography.   I. Title.
    GV1785.G7A3 1991
    792.8'028'092—dc20   91-15444
    [B]   CIP

ISBN 0-385-26503-4

10 9 8 7 6 5 4 3 2 1

FIRST EDITION

"And the lot of the purple and scarlet fell to Mary."

—THE PROTO EVANGELIUM JACOBI
Chapter 10, verse 2
2nd century A.D.

To my mother and father, to Geordie, Mary, Lizzie, and William Henry.

To Ron Protas, my friend who worked with me and shared a new direction and animation for my life.

To my editor, Jacqueline Onassis, whose faith made this book a reality.

To Howard Kaplan for his dedication and sensitivity during our many hours together in preparing this book.

To Halston, who helped me as a collaborator and became my hands. To Liza Minnelli and Mikhail Baryshnikov, who gave me of their gifts as artists and of their spirits as my loving friends.

To the distinguished chairmen of our board: Francis Mason, who helped us start up again, Lee Traub, Arnold Weissberger, Judith Schlosser, and Evelyn Sharp, who joined us to go on.

To my beloved Alice Tully and to my friend and counselor Frances Wickes.

To Linda Hodes, Yuriko, Helen O'Brien, Maureen Musialek, and Christopher Herrmann, who have strengthened my resolve and ability to go on.

To all of my dancers, past, present and future . . .

January 1991

BLOOD MEMORY

I am a dancer.

I believe that we learn by practice. Whether it means to learn to dance by practicing dancing or to learn to live by practicing living, the principles are the same. In each it is the performance of a dedicated precise set of acts, physical or intellectual, from which comes shape of achievement, a sense of one's being, a satisfaction of spirit. One becomes in some area an athlete of God.

To practice means to perform, in the face of all obstacles, some act of vision, of faith, of desire. Practice is a means of inviting the perfection desired.

I think the reason dance has held such an ageless magic for the world is that it has been the symbol of the performance of living. Even as I write, time has begun to make today yesterday—the past. The most brilliant scientific discoveries will in time change and perhaps grow obsolete, as new scientific manifestations emerge. But art is eternal, for it reveals the inner landscape, which is the soul of man.

Many times I hear the phrase "the dance of life." It is an expression that touches me deeply, for the instrument through which the dance speaks is also the instrument through which life is lived—the human body. It is the instrument by which all the primaries of life are made manifest. It holds in its memory all matters of life and death and love. Dancing appears glamorous, easy, delightful. But the path to the paradise of the achievement is not easier than any other. There is fatigue so great that the body cries, even in its sleep. There are times of complete frustration, there are daily small deaths. Then I need all the comfort that practice has stored in my memory, a tenacity of faith.

It takes about ten years to make a mature dancer. The training is twofold. First comes the study and practice of the craft which is the school where you are working in order to strengthen the muscular structure of the body. The body is shaped, disciplined, honored, and in time, trusted. The movement becomes clean, precise, eloquent, truthful. Movement never lies. It is a barometer telling the state of the soul's weather to all who can read it. This might be called the law of the dancer's life—the law which governs its outer aspects.

Then comes the cultivation of the being from which whatever you have to say comes. It doesn't just come out of nowhere, it comes out of a great curiosity. The main thing, of course, always is the fact that there is only one of you in the world, just one, and if that is not fulfilled then something has been lost. Ambition is not enough; necessity is everything. It is through this that the legends of the soul's journey are retold with all their tragedy and their bitterness and sweetness of living. It is at this point that the sweep of life catches up with the mere personality of the performer, and while the individual becomes greater, the personal becomes less personal. And there is grace. I mean the grace resulting from faith . . . faith in life, in love, in people, in the act of dancing. All this is necessary to any performance in life which is magnetic, powerful, rich in meaning.

In a dancer, there is a reverence for such forgotten things as the miracle of the small beautiful bones and their delicate strength. In a thinker, there is a reverence for the beauty of the alert and directed and lucid mind. In all of us who perform there is an awareness of the smile which is part of the equipment, or gift, of the acrobat. We have all walked the high wire of circumstance at times. We recognize the gravity pull of the earth as he does. The smile is there because he is practicing living at that instant of danger. He does not choose to fall.

At times I fear walking that tightrope. I fear the venture into the unknown. But that is part of the act of creating and the act of performing. That is what a dancer does.

People have asked me why I chose to be a dancer. I did not choose. I was chosen to be a dancer, and with that, you live all your life. When any young student asks me, "Do you think I should be a dancer?" I always say, "If you have to ask, then the answer is no." Only if there is one way to make life vivid for yourself and for others should you embark upon such a career . . . You will know the wonders of the human body because there is nothing more wonderful. The next time you look into the mirror, just look at the way the ears rest next to the head; look at the way the hairline grows; think of all the little bones in your wrist. It is a miracle. And the dance is a celebration of that miracle.

I feel that the essence of dance is the expression of man—the landscape of his soul. I hope that every dance I do reveals something of myself or some wonderful thing a human being can be. It is the unknown—whether it is the myths or the legends or the rituals that give us our memories. It is the eternal pulse of life, the utter desire. I know that when we have rehearsals, and we have them every day, there are some dancers, particularly men, who cannot be still. One of the men in my company is not built to be still. He has to be moving. I think at times he does not know what he is doing, but that is another matter. He's got the essence of a man's inner life that prods him to dance. He has that desire. Every dance is a kind of fever chart, a graph of the heart. Desire is a lovely thing, and that is where the dance comes from, from desire.

Each day of rehearsal for a new ballet I arrive at a little before two in the afternoon, and sit alone in my studio to have a moment of stillness before the dancers enter. I tease myself and say I am cultivating my Buddha nature; but it is really just such a comforting place for me to be—secure, clear, and with a purpose. It is that order of these elements together that led one writer to call dance "glorified human behavior." I sit with my back to our large mirrors so that I am completely within myself. The room is a bit of a jumble; we are to leave on tour soon. Packing crates are lined up with those pieces Isamu Noguchi made for me that will travel with us, stenciled in black: APPALACHIAN SPRING, HÉRODIADE, NIGHT JOURNEY.

This studio with its worn floors, and its door that opens into the garden, means the world to me. When Lila Acheson Wallace presented it to me in 1952 it was a security to know I could work and have a home. Lila was a glorious being. She understood the divine turbulence within an artist, and had a way of supporting you without ever making you feel beholden or awkward.

I can never forget my first visit to her home, High Winds. When we

6

sat at the dining room table, Lila drank from a beautiful gold cup, given to her by the Egyptian government, which she told me came from Tutankhamen's tomb. Lila's husband, DeWitt, looked at me and said, "So, you're a dancer." He lifted his hand over my head and asked, "Can you kick this?" It was a formal evening, and I was wearing a Dior. I answered, "I can, but not in this dress." The memories of Lila visiting me here and giving me her acts of light as a friend often return to me in this studio; and other moments as well. They say that energy, once it is created and enters the world, can never be destroyed, it only changes. Perhaps that is why I sense so many presences in this room.

Outside my studio door, in my garden, is a tree that has always been a symbol of facing life, and in many ways it is a dancer. It began as a sapling when I first moved here and although a wire gate was in its way, it persisted and grew to the light, and now thirty years later it is a tree with a very thick trunk, with the wire embedded within. Like a dancer it went to the light and carried the scars of its journey inside. You traverse, you work, you make it right. You embody within yourself that curiosity, use that avidity for life no matter whether it is for good or for evil. The body is a sacred garment. It's your first and your last garment; it is what you enter life in and what you depart life with, and it should be treated with honor, and with joy and with fear as well. But always, though, with blessing.

They say that the two primary arts were dance and architecture. The word "theatre" was a verb before it was a noun—an act, then a place. That means you must make the gesture, the effort, the real effort to communicate with another being. And you also must have a tree to shelter under in case of storm or sun. There is always that tree, that creative force, and there is always a house, a theatre.

Trees can be the most beautiful things in the world, particularly when they are not in leaf. There is one tree where the road cuts through Central Park from the East to the West Side. Each passage I make during the

7

seasons shows it in a different aspect of becoming. When it is out of leaf, it becomes so old and so striking, rather like my favorite No mask, of an old woman who had once been very beautiful. Each time I see that tree I salute it for its power, and its mystery.

The spine is your body's tree of life. And through it a dancer communicates; his body says what words cannot, and if he is pure and open, he can make of his body a tragical instrument.

That tension, that intensification of a body in its stillness and in its movement, I feel reflected in our studio. At one time a creek ran through this property, and I believe the land still holds some of that hidden water. The Greeks felt that where there was a spring, a manifestation of the flow of life, there also was a goddess who could either be placated or offended. It is a strange force that at times seems alive under our building. Even in the studio, we have had a little shoot of plant life come up out of the floor just near the piano. It is another world and we accept it as a gift.

I am absorbed in the magic of movement and light. Movement never lies. It is the magic of what I call the outer space of the imagination. There is a great deal of outer space, distant from our daily lives, where I feel our imagination wanders sometimes. It will find a planet or it will not find a planet, and that is what a dancer does.

And then there is inspiration. Where does it come from? Mostly from the excitement of living. I get it from the diversity of a tree or the ripple of the sea, a bit of poetry, the sighting of a dolphin breaking the still water and moving toward me . . . anything that quickens you to the instant. And whether one would call that inspiration or necessity, I really do not know. At times I receive that inspiration from people; I enjoy people very much and for the most part feel it is returned. I simply happen to love people. I do not love them all individually, but I love the idea of life pulsing through people—blood and movement.

For all of us, but particularly for a dancer with his intensification of life and his body, there is a blood memory that can speak to us. Each of us from our mother and father has received their blood and through their parents and their parents' parents and backward into time. We carry thousands of years of that blood and its memory. How else to explain those instinctive gestures and thoughts that come to us, with little preparation or expectation. They come perhaps from some deep memory of a time when the world was chaotic, when, as the Bible says, the world was nothing. And then, as if some door opened slightly, there was light. It revealed certain wonderful things. It revealed terrifying things. But it was light.

William Goyen, in *The House of Breath*, wrote that "we are the carriers of lives and legends—who knows the unseen frescoes on the private walls of the skull." Very often making a dance springs from a desire to find those hidden frescoes.

In Burma, on our second Asian tour in the 1970s, I had been asked to present flowers at the tomb of the Burmese Unknown Soldier. This I did in the presence of our ambassador and the Burmese minister of culture. When I had finished, there was a tremendous stir, great sounds of conversation. The Burmese wanted to know who had coached me to present the flowers in precisely the correct manner, steps, and gestures that would be appropriate to a Burmese woman of my age and station. No one had. Just as no one had taught Ruth St. Denis to touch back generations in East Indian dance to find the true path and spirit for her solos which even the Indians at that time had lost.

But for this you must keep your vessel clean—your mind, your body; it is what the Zen masters tell their students who get too full of themselves, too wrapped up in theory and too many thoughts. They ask them, "That is all very good; but have you cleaned your dish?" For the Buddhist student lived by begging food; and how could he receive it if his bowl was not clean? He is being asked if he is ready for his next meal. A clear instruction to get back to basics. It is so easy to become cluttered.

I think that is what my father must have meant when he wrote to me when I was away from home. "Martha," he said, "you must keep an open soul."

It is that openness and awareness and innocence of sorts that I try to cultivate in my dancers. Although, as the Latin verb to educate, *educere*, indicates, it is not a question of putting something in but drawing it out, if it is there to begin with.

As our rehearsal begins, I will mention that sensitivity and openness. The dancers enter with associate directors Linda Hodes and Ron Protas, whom I have trained over the years to oversee my works and to whom I have entrusted the future of my company. Linda came to me as a child, trained with me, and danced with me onstage. Ron has been with me for twenty-five years and I have trained him in my technique. He knows deeply the roles I have created and can intuit what I want. There are always one or two dancers missing—an injury, a therapy session, the usual. Dancers today can do anything; the technique is phenomenal. The passion and the meaning to their movement can be another thing.

At times I will tease my dancers and tell them that perhaps they are not too bright today, that all of their jumping has addled their brains. And yet they move with grace and a kind of inevitability, some more powerfully than others. This moment of rehearsal is the instant that I care about. This is the very now of my life.

The only thing we have is the now. You begin from the now, what you know, and move into the old, ancient ones that you did not know but which you find as you go along. I think you only find the past from yourself, from what you're experiencing now, what enters your life at the present moment. We don't know about the past, except as we discover it. And we discover it from the now. Looking at the past is like lolling in a rocking chair. It is so relaxing and you can rock back and forth on the porch, and never go forward. It is not for me. People sometimes ask me about retirement and I say, "Retire? Retire into what?" I don't believe in retirement because that is the time you die.

The life of a dancer is by no means simple. It is comparatively short. I am not an example of that, but I could not do certain things beyond a certain point. Old age is a pain in the neck. I didn't want to grow old

because I didn't realize that I was growing old. I feel that it is a burden and a fearful thing and one I have to endure. It is not a thing to be treasured or to be loved. It is by any means a difficulty to bear.

When I stopped dancing, it was not a conscious decision. I realized that I did not have the strength or the ability to build into the interior and the soul of the artist. Before I began to dance I trained myself to do four hundred jumps in five minutes by the clock. Today, there are so many things I can't do. I get absolutely furious that I cannot do them. I didn't want to stop dancing and still do not want to. I have always wanted a simple, direct, open, clean, and wonderful life. That has been my time.

There are always ancestral footsteps behind me, pushing me, when I am creating a new dance, and gestures are flowing through me. Whether good or bad, they are ancestral. You get to the point where your body is something else and it takes on a world of cultures from the past, an idea that is very hard to express in words. I never verbalize about the dance as I create it. It is a purely physical risk that you desire to take, and that you have to take. The ballet I am doing now is a risk. That is all I can say because it isn't fulfilled yet. I let no one watch, except for the dancers I am working with. When they leave I am alone with the ancestral footsteps.

Somewhere very long ago I remember hearing that in El Greco's studio, after he died, they found an empty canvas on which he had written only three words: "Nothing pleases me." This I can understand.

At moments I think that it is time for me to stop. I think of Mallarmé's image of the swan, the beautiful swan, who stayed too long in the winter water until the ice closed around his feet, and he was caught. I wonder, sometimes, if I have stayed too long. Perhaps I am just being afraid.

The American Indians thought that life existed in recurring cycles of death and renewal. Now I wonder if I am to begin a new cycle or if it is part depression, which is a part of doing anything. It is a part of the glory and part of the inevitability, the unknowing part as well.

I have rehearsals and I teach class. I travel with my company whenever I can and sit in the wings, usually with Ron, and give corrections that he takes down on his yellow pad. In the audience Linda and another rehearsal director do the same. And then the dancers receive their corrections.

Sometimes the dancers are fine and I say that they are. But sometimes they are not. They are offensive to the form of the piece. There are departures that are made, liberties that are taken, and I have to say no. I conduct the rehearsals and I demonstrate, and I teach class. It all comes down to this: if you put your name on something you should be there.

There is also the vital business of fund-raising. It is very much necessary. In today's world you can do nothing without money. You can have your dreams. You can have the image in your soul, but you cannot objectify it without the means. I rest insecure, not knowing whether my works will be filmed and preserved and whether we can meet the mortgage for our building. There is no Halston, no Lila to stand with me now and to help me. And yet Madonna, one of my former students, has entered our lives and has talked with me and says we will find a way.

There are times when I return to my home near my school after teaching a particularly difficult class and I wonder where all the loveliness, all the awareness of the magic of the body, has gone. I think of the many times I've experienced certain strange happenings. Some were tales told to me by my parents, and some I remember. Always it seems to me that I was aware of a great curiosity about life, about the actions of other people, other beings. Something of what Empedocles speaks of when he says, "For I have been, ere now, a boy and a girl, a bush, a bird, a dumb fish in the sea." In other words some drops of memory of those past identifications flood over me—not reincarnation or transformation or anything of the kind. I'm speaking of the divinity of memory, the fragments of a memory, and those things of great value that we forget and that the body and the mind choose to remember . . . Emily Dickinson's "intuition picks up the key that memory drops."

What I miss some days in a dance class is not perfection, because some of them will never achieve that moment of technical expertise. I don't demand, at the beginning, any vestige of perfection. What I long for is the eagerness to meet life, the curiosity, the wonder that you feel when you can really move—to work toward a perfect first or a perfect fifth position. There becomes an excitement, an avidity, a forgetfulness of everyone about you. You are so completely absorbed in this instrument that is vibrant to life. The great French poet St. John Perse said to me, "You have so little time to be born to the instant." This I miss in class very much. I miss the animal strength, the beauty of the heel as it is used to carry one forward into life. This, I think more than anything, is the secret of my loneliness.

I do not feel myself unique by any means, but I do know that I agree with Edgard Varèse—and I'm going to use a word that I never use regarding myself or anybody else. And that word is genius. Varèse, a wonderful French composer, who wrote some music for me, opened up new areas of musical strength in the way he used percussion that I had never experienced before. He said, "Martha, all of us are born with genius, but most people only keep it for a few seconds."

By genius he meant that curiosity that leads to the search for the secret of life. That is what tires me when I teach and I come away alone. Sometimes you will see a person on the stage who has this oneness with himself—it is so glorious it has the power to stop you. It is a common gift to all of us but most people only keep it a few moments.

I can never forget the evening I was staying late at the school, and the phone rang. I was the only one there and I picked it up to hear a mother ask about classes for her child. "She is a genius. Intuitive. Unique. It must be nurtured now." "Really," I answered. "And how old is she?" Her mother replied, "Two years old." I told her that we only accepted children at nine (today much earlier, thanks to vitamins and computers and home training). "Nine!" she cried. "But by nine she will have lost all of her genius." I said, "Madame, if she must lose it, it is best she lose it young."

I never thought of myself as being what they call a genius. I don't know what genius is. I think a far better expression is a retriever, a lovely strong golden retriever that brings things back from the past, or retrieves things from our common blood memory. I think that by every act you do—whether in religion, politics, or sex—you reveal yourself. This, to me, is one of the wonderful things in life. It is what I've always wanted to do—to show the laughing, the fun, the appetite, all of it through dance.

In order to work, in order to be excited, in order to simply be, you have to be reborn to the instant. You have to permit yourself to feel, you have to permit yourself to be vulnerable. You may not like what you see, that is not important. You don't always have to judge. But you must be attacked by it, excited by it, and your body must be alive. And you must know how to animate that body; for each it is individual. I remember the great Russian ballet teacher Volkova, who had fled during the Russian Revolution and was teaching in Denmark. Interestingly enough, she never learned a word of Danish, only English. A young man did a series of extraordinary leaps across the floor. He looked back at Volkova for the praise he knew was his, and she said, "It was perfect. But too effective."

When a dancer is at the peak of his power he has two lovely, fragile, and perishable things. One is the spontaneity that is arrived at over years of training. The other is simplicity, but not the usual kind. It is the state of complete simplicity costing no less than absolutely everything, of which T. S. Eliot speaks.

How many leaps did Nijinsky take before he made the one that startled the world? He took thousands and thousands and it is that legend that gives us the courage, the energy, and arrogance to go back into the studio knowing that while there is so little time to be born to the instant, you will work again among the many that you may once more be born as one. That is a dancer's world.

My dancer's world has seen so many theatres, so many instants. But always I have resisted looking backward until now, when I began to sense that there was always for my life a line through it—necessity. The Greek myths speak of the spindle of life resting on the knee of necessity, the principal Fate in the Platonic world. The second Fate weaves, and the third cuts. Necessity to create? No. But in some way to transcend, to conquer fear, to find a way to go on.

How does it all begin? I suppose it never begins. It just continues.

A few years ago the newspaper published a list of hundreds of names, owners of unclaimed property held by a bank. The paper listed a safety deposit box I had taken over twenty-five years ago. The bank wanted two hundred dollars or they were going to take the contents to auction. My assistant went to Brooklyn to recover it. Inside, no cash or jewelry, but

At the age of two, a willful child.

insurance policies and personal papers, an application for a Guggenheim fellowship, which I later won. Also, a piece of paper that traced my family generations back to Miles Standish and Plymouth Rock —my family tree.

In 1894, Grover Cleveland was in his second presidential term, Alfred Dreyfus was condemned for treason in France, and Claude Debussy composed *L'Après-midi d'un faune*. Victoria was still Queen. During the second week in May my mother began her labor, and on the eleventh I was born.

My childhood years were a balance of light and dark. Allegheny, Pennsylvania, was completely bleak, and lacking in life, brightness, and any discernible beauty. The coal industry was dominant and everything we wore was eventually covered in soot. Soot everywhere—on window boxes, doors, trees. To go outside in a freshly washed white dress was to return home covered in black. It seemed as if we were constantly doing a wash in our house. All the women and all of the girls in town wore veils. We had to because of the coal. And gloves because of the soot and because they were proper.

I remember walking on Main Street as a young girl, a veil covering my eyes, my nose, and my mouth. My view of the world was made pretty by the sheer fabric, the very mystery of the netting. Strangers would come up to me on the street and lift my veil to kiss me on the cheek. This is how children were greeted by adults. Of course, I would not let them. My father disapproved and told me I must not let anyone kiss me on the face. There was a lot of illness around due to the nature of our industrial environment. He instructed me to say, "My father, Dr. Graham, will not permit anyone to kiss me on the face, but you may kiss my hand."

When I got older I thought gloves were a way of hiding something. I still don't like gloves, but I wear them. My hands are not beautiful, now bent and gnarled from arthritis. I try to keep them in a kind of form that gloves permit. Children, especially, do not like it when I wear gloves. They don't want to touch me. And they don't want me to touch them. I can understand it because they don't really meet me. I'm withholding something from them. I wear gloves to meet people and I wear them to go outside.

When my father was not in consultation with a patient, I would haunt his office, careful not to disturb his work. It was quite a serious place, a great wonder to me as a child, lined with books that provoked my curiosity. It felt different from any room I had ever been in. I remember standing on a great pile of books to reach the height of my father's desk. He showed me a glass slide on which he had placed a drop of water. He held the slide in his hand between his thumb and index finger and said, "Martha, what do you see?" I said, simply enough, "Water." And he said, "Pure water?" I said, "I think so. Pure water." I thought my father was acting a bit strange and I did not know what he was getting at. Then, from a high shelf over his desk, he removed a microscope and placed it near me. He adjusted the window shade to give the moment the proper light and placed the slide of water on his microscope. I squinted one eye closed and brought the other to the heavy black lens. Then I saw the contents of the slide of water and said to my father in horror, "But there are wriggles in it!" He said, "Yes, it is impure. Just remember this all of your life, Martha. You must look for the truth." Look for the truth, whatever that truth may be— good, bad, or unsettling.

19

I have never forgotten the vividness of that moment, which has presided like a star over my life. In a curious way, this was my first dance lesson—a gesture toward the truth.

George G. Graham, M.D.

My dashing father, "Goldie" Graham, and his calling card.

When my father was in with a patient and others were waiting, I would sit nearby to see how they moved; sometimes I'd tell them stories. I don't think they welcomed either my attendance or my inventions. One particular patient, a seventeen-year-old woman, was invited to supper with us. When we were all seated at the dining room table, we bowed our heads and Grandmother said grace.

Oddly enough, Father's patient said little, and as I recall barely looked up from her plate, preferring to sit slightly slouched, bent into that awkwardness, as if folding herself into her own body, that difficult habit of self. I don't remember the dinner conversation, only this young woman's behavior. She appeared fidgety, a bit nervous. I'd look at my father, but his look, in kindness, gave no clue to her behavior. Later, after my father had accompanied her back to her own home, I asked him why she behaved in this way, and he replied that she was not well, and her body was telling us so. Each of us tells our own story even without speaking. "Movement," he later told me when I asked more questions, "never lies."

My father George Greenfield Graham was a doctor of nervous disorders, what in those days was known as an alienist, and what today would be called a psychiatrist. His father was a banker, the first president of the Bank of Pittsburgh, who, as soon as my father was born, established a trust fund in his name. This enabled him to go to college and medical school, and on this money, I was raised as well. And it was because of those factories and my father's work in medicine that Lizzie entered our family.

Lizzie was an institution in all our lives. It seems that she was brought over from Ireland by some well-to-do family when she was quite young. One day, she was attacked by a pack of wild dogs and was very badly bitten. She was taken to the local hospital, where my father treated her. She was close to death from the toxicity of her wounds, but my father pulled her through. She felt eternally grateful to him and promised that when he had a wife and child she would come back and take care of them. Time passed, several years, and it was forgotten.

One day, my mother was holding me in her arms, trying to calm me. She must have been distraught as I was an uneasy child. My mother was very young, very pretty, and inexperienced in taking care of a house, a husband,

Lizzie.

My nurse, Lizzie Prendergast.

and raising a child. My father was away from home often, making his various calls and rounds, and she must have spent a great deal of her time alone. The brass knocker rapped, and my mother answered the door with me in her arms. On the doorstep stood this young woman, a fresh Irish girl. She said, "I am Lizzie. I have come to take care of the doctor and his family." My mother took one look at both of us, held me out to her, and said, "Here, take her."

That began the reign of Lizzie in our house. She moved in and stayed there as a member of our family until she died, years later when I was in the *Greenwich Village Follies*. Her rule was absolute. She was not educated. She was wise and she was utterly dedicated and devoted—particularly to my father who had saved her life.

And so there I was with Lizzie, a wonderful lapsed Catholic who could never understand why she had to go to confession. "What do I have to confess?" she'd ask. Lizzie, whom I could run to when my double-jointed arm would go out and say, "Lizzie, pull. Pull." And she would and all would be well. Lizzie, who recoiled in horror when she came to my high school play where I was performing Dido, and at the climactic moment when I took a knife to my side, jumped up and cried, "Martha, put down that knife, you'll hurt yourself!"

My sister Mary in Mother's arms, and me on Father's knee, late 1890s.

The birth of my sister Mary came at a time when I felt an extreme stillness in our home. I don't recall for how many days this enveloped us. My mother was upstairs in her room, and my father and grandmother were constantly at her call and her attendance. Up my father would go with a pitcher of cold water, and down my grandmother would come with a tray of food barely touched, or a wicker basket of damp cloths. I was in the main room downstairs. I felt there was something in the house being born, or another presence in the house upstairs, and I suddenly became very frightened. It was then that my grandmother took a great metal poker from the fireplace and began to bang on the andirons. I did not know what to make of this—the first sound that I can remember.

When my grandmother stopped it was quiet in the top part of the house, and my father walked slowly down the stairs toward me and said, "Martha, you now have a sister. We have named her Mary. Would you like to meet her?" I do not know if I said yes immediately—I was becoming quite stubborn and willful even then—but I did take his hand and together we climbed the stairs. This was two years after I was born. My next sister, Georgia, was born four years after her. My father felt that only in that time could my mother gain enough strength in her womb to carry and birth another child. Though my father was a doctor, he did not deliver the children. He felt that he was too emotional and that he could not do it the way it should be done, so he had a friend, a fellow doctor, oversee the labor and deliver the children.

My mother weighed less than one hundred pounds, and my father used to carry her around the house and up the stairs, her curly hair cascading down about his arms. She was a very delicate woman. She took to the adoration of her husband very well. I believe they loved and respected one another very much. Mother's relationship to our father was almost like a child's. She was treasured because she was so little, so young and beautiful. Theirs was a warm, strong relationship and it had nothing to do with women's liberation, which she didn't understand. She wanted to be her husband's wife.

There was a deep and tender courting and love between my parents. Two of his letters to her in Allegheny, in 1891, before they were married, make me almost tearful now when I read them, and I am not one to cry. He begins one letter "My dear little Jean," and another, "My dearest Jeannie" and, oh, the warmth of those letters. He writes:

23

I am awfully sorry that I cannot go and see you as I intended but please accept of the floral offering, and love me until Saturday, at least, when I hope to see you. Please write to me if nothing more than one word of love. No one can tell how much I thirst for the one sight of your dear face. . . .

I will wait until then. Kisses. George.

They married on April 23, 1893.

24

My great-grandmother tried to make proper young ladies out of all of us, which never really interested me. She used to sit in a big chair on the side porch of the house, and as a child I was completely stunned by the fact that anybody could be so old. What I had to do to please her was show her that I knew how to iron a beautiful handkerchief. This was my responsibility, the job that she had given to me, rather than to Geordie or to Mary. I was the eldest and this was my task. I had to wash and then press each one with a cast-iron contraption we had to heat up over the fire, and constantly reheat, in order to make it suitable to remove the wrinkles from the cotton cloth. I would finish this chore, then present a pile of warm, what I thought to be perfectly ironed handkerchiefs to my great-grandmother for her examination. If one of them was not to her liking—if it was not perfectly ironed— she would snap it open, dip it in a glass of water, and I had to iron it again. She was trying to make me into a proper young lady, an idea which thoroughly bored me. But out of respect,

My great-grandmother, on whom I based the character of the Ancestress in Letter to the World.

I followed her instructions. I still remember her admonition, "I would rather have a man with bad morals than with bad manners."

We were brought up to be ladies, with the plan that one day we would be wives. What else was there except a wife? You were supposed to marry and have children and so on. You were brought up in that fashion and you were expected to behave that way.

I did not know my paternal grandmother. She attended Vassar, where my father always hoped I would study. We kept a portrait of Grandmother in the house, with my father standing to her side. I still have it. She wore eyeglasses and he wore little blue pants and a little blue shirt. I thought the entire outfit to be very elegant, though I got the impression my father found the entire thing a silly ordeal; he was pouting. I imagine it was some person, some itinerant man who went from house to house and painted portraits of various ladies and their children.

My attitude toward Mother became one of adoration and care, but never petition. I never tried to get things out of her. Never. We were not supposed to intrude upon anything that she had. Her dressing table was sacrosanct. You did not touch anything on that dressing table—not a piece of candy, nothing.

When I was no longer living at home, but on my own and out of my mother's aura, I would send her a telegram or a note or whatever I could on my birthday. It always said, "On this, my birthday, thank you for my life."

Years later, women in the movement would claim me as a women's liberationist. But I never think of myself in this way. I was never aware of it, because I have never felt competition. I was brought up in a very strange way. I have been surrounded by men all my life so the movement really didn't touch me. But I never had the feeling that I was inferior. So when this all began in the last twenty or so years I was baffled by it. I had no affiliation with it, and I always got whatever I wanted from men without asking.

My father had a lot to do with this attitude. He always made it necessary that I be who I was. Once, after giving a performance, I was approached by a woman who asked me about my role in the women's liberation movement. I looked at her and said, "My father raised me to be a woman."

There was a woman in Austria who insisted I was such a strong female figure that I must have had girlfriends. I said, "It is impossible. I have no interest in women. I like men." If I had wanted that kind of life with a woman I would have had it. I did not. I wanted a life with men and that is what I chose.

All the things I do are in every woman. Every woman is a Medea. Every woman is a Jocasta. There comes a time when every woman is mother to her husband. Clytemnestra is every woman when she kills. In most of the ballets I have done, the woman has absolutely and completely triumphed. Why this is so I do not really know, except that I am a woman. I know that in a woman, like a lioness, is the urge to kill if she cannot have what she wants. Much more so than in a man. Woman kills, intends to kill. She is more ruthless than any man.

You do what you have to do, I suppose. You do what is attractive and wonderful to you at the time. That's why I did women like Clytemnestra. It comes out of that deep desire for creation. One girl came to me and said, "But I am not Clytemnestra. I would never kill anyone."

"On the contrary," I said, "I have seen you look at a man in such a way that you have killed him right there on the spot. If that is not murder, just as the other, then I do not understand it."

After a few moments of silence she looked at me and said, "I think you're right."

I tried to show the three aspects of all women in *El Penitente*, my ballet of 1940. Every woman who is worth anything has some of these in her. Every woman has that quality of being a virgin, of being the temptress-prostitute, of being the mother. I feel that these, more than anything, are the common life of all women. Not politics.

26

William Henry Graham, my brother.

.   .   .

My mother delivered four children—three girls and one boy, who died early of meningitis. He was just a baby. I remember the day he was baptized in an upstairs room in our house. My father was ecstatic because he had always wanted a son. Eighteen months after his birth, this boy-child, William Henry Graham, died of scarlet fever. William Henry was baptized in a cut-glass crystal bowl that was my grandmother's and now sits in the vitrine in my living room.

I remember how father used to recite stories to us from the Greek myths. My days would be filled with these tales, these word paintings, and sometimes, before sleep, he would fill my imagination with thoughts of these people who only exist in the realm of story. I remember how he told the story of Achilles and how his mother dipped him in water, as if it were a baptism. Well, perhaps it was a baptism that became, for him, a kind of living, vital shield. I remember thinking about the error of the foot, how it was his heel, some small part of the body, that became his undoing. I wanted to redip him into the water to protect him.

.   .   .

I was quite young when animals entered my life, and from what I recall and what my mother and father later told me, they entered in a rather enormous way. I was evidently still in diapers when my parents took me to the circus for the first time. I was completely overwhelmed by the activity, all the lives around and above me, the impossibilities of the various actions—barker, acrobat, clown. But I was truly stunned when it came time to view the animals. One particular elephant, chained, stood in an area with his keeper that had been cordoned off by ropes. Somehow in the tumult and terrific excitement, I managed to elude both my mother and father. Each thought that the other had me tightly held, but I wriggled free, crawled over what felt like dirt and sawdust, slipped under the ropes and made directly for the elephant. It was the most strange and fascinating thing that I had ever beheld. His large, slow, wet eyes looked down to where I was—his very wink was like slowly falling curtains. His great trunk began to sway when suddenly my father, realizing what had happened, reached over in terror to pick me up by the seat of my pants and drag me back. The elephant's keeper saw what was happening and immediately ran over and said breathlessly to my father, "You should not have done that. The animal would never have hurt the child, but he would have probably killed you."

After this, I doubt if my parents took me back to the circus, much less let me out of their sight. But in that brief moment I made contact with something alive but not human. Something, in its own way, mysterious and worldly. Animals became very special beings for me. Later on in my life I would again come face to face with an elephant.

This happened in Ceylon, when my company and I were on our way to see the Kandy dancers with our guide and sponsor, impresario Donovan Andre. We were all extremely fatigued from the heat and the company was bored. We had arrived at an outdoor theatre, a place of vast rock carvings and human mystery. There was a rice paddy, dry at that time of year, and across this was a very small, but hidden, temple. It had no roof but it had some very strange and beautiful wood carvings, particularly one of a woman similar to a carving I have in my home now. It had sat in the rain so long that she had become desiccated and almost a symbol of existing life.

The dancers wandered elsewhere, leaving me alone. Suddenly, I heard footsteps. I knew they weren't human footsteps, so I turned very slowly. Slowly, heavily, a great elephant was approaching me. I was alone. He was alone. I could not move. I had no command of the situation. He came and looked down with his strong, weighty eyes. I looked up at him and I said to myself, "If this is it, this is it. There is no place to run."

The elephant came up to me very slowly and stood over me, not with his legs over me, but with his head—that great head bending down toward me and those wonderful eyes looking into mine. We went on like this, staring at each other, for what seemed like a bit of forever. Then he turned, shuffled back, and just went off into the jungle with his tail swinging. He did not touch me. I felt that in some way I had met a person or a friend, somebody out of my past and it was a very awesome and treasured experience. The very walk, the back of the elephant, the thin swinging tail, those flapping great ears. It was a creature from another world, and so are all the creatures in the imagination of our minds.

Elephants have always been very special beings for me and I have always felt an affiliation with them. Today, I am involved in saving the elephants from extinction, from people who would kill them for the beauty of their tusks for adornment or display—that living ivory. It is one of the reasons that I am a vegetarian today. As a child, however, I enjoyed meat, potatoes, and all vegetables. But today no meat, no fish, nothing of the kind. Animals exist as a power, as an entity in themselves. Animals deserve to live. They are very, very beautiful. Deserving to live is a pretty terrific thing. An animal exhibits his desire to live most of his days.

No animal ever has an ugly body until it is domesticated. It is the same with the human body. Civilization has made it impossible and undesirable for us to lead the rugged lives of our ancestors, but in the place of physical adventure, which kept them alert, alive to the very fingertips, we have a hundredfold more mental adventures, which serve the same purpose of quickening our pulses and vitalizing our energies. To those who can become as openminded as children the dance has a tremendous power. It is a spiritual touchstone.

Some afternoons Lizzie would take me to the park, but even during the afternoon, Pittsburgh was dark, as if the city was spun entirely out of evening and dark thread. One day, we came across swans in the pond. There was one black swan I thought was very beautiful. We stood at the edge of the water, and much to Lizzie's dismay, I waved my handkerchief at him, until he came close enough to be able to snatch it out of my hand. He seemed to be an animal of pure throat and gleaming feathers, and of course, as I soon learned, one terrific bite. Lizzie put me on the other side of her to separate me from the black swan. "You leave those swans alone," she said. "They are evil."

The elusive aspects of the black swan have always held me fast. The black swan can hypnotize you—perhaps because of its snakelike neck and cobra swaying. Its neck, with its quality of fluid movement, is so beautiful but as deadly as a weapon. I believe Petipa must have studied swans for his *Swan Lake*. To witness the swan in water spinning into itself, you can understand the fouettés he created for the Black Swan. And in nature it is the black swan that is the most dangerous. If there is such a thing as reincarnation, I would like to come back to dance the Black Swan. The only change I would like in the production would be the image of Rotbart, the magician who controls all of the swans. I don't see him as a monstrous creature as he is so often portrayed, but as a beautiful, handsome man, perfectly dressed. He would have the power to seduce every woman, every swan that approached him. Sexuality is still the most powerful lure and manipulation.

·   ·   ·

During my early years in Pittsburgh my father and mother would take trips to California to scout out future homes for us. They would leave Lizzie in command, and Lizzie's word was law. My sisters and I had a large nursery with wooden blocks which we would build into cities— practical houses with windows, doors, and all those sorts of things. I felt that this play with blocks, this fantasy with blocks, this making of another landscape which could be called livable, contributed a great deal to what is now called choreography. I never saw a dance performance in Pittsburgh. Dance wasn't even heard of. I'm not speaking now of dancing. That's an entirely different part of the art of the dance. I'm not speaking of the technique. I'm speaking of the stage planning and the presentation of a story, an idea, or an emotion in formal terms, as one uses the words of a language to present a poem, a letter, or any thought which passes through one's mind. Lizzie dominated the house at this time. She used to sit on the floor with us. She had a sweet, lovely voice and would sing songs to us, the current musicals of the time. She was a devotee of the theatre.

I was a child and had never been inside a theatre, but Lizzie had and brought to my imagination her descriptions of both the stage and the song that accompanied it. The playroom was our first theatre, as we constructed elaborate stories and built cities from blocks of wood. It was Lizzie whose job it was to protect Mary, Geordie, and me, by forming a barrier to the world on one side. But on the other side, she created a great and wonderful release for us. I remember one of her songs, from a musical of the time. It began, "I'm only a bird in a gilded cage, a beautiful sight to see." Another one, which left little marks on my memory but which I have forgotten until the beginning of now, went like this:

Waltz me around again Willie
'Round, 'round, 'round.
Music so dreamy
It's peaches and creamy
And don't let my feet touch the ground.

Music, then, became important for our small theatres. Once I surprised Mary, Geordie, and Lizzie by inviting them into my room at a specific time of day to attend a show I had created. For a curtain I rigged a bed sheet from one end of the room to the other. When the curtain was drawn, I was alone singing the following song. It was my big number:

Idaho, oh whoa, don't go so fast, dear,
My horse won't last, dear,
So won't you please go slow.

My mother was an extraordinary woman in that she saw and responded to the fact that her children were theatrically inclined, although we had never been to a theatre. So she made us little dresses with trains and we had all the junky jewelry that we wanted to play with. My sisters and I played dress-up all the time. We used veils, scarves, anything that was theatrical in that sense.

I always loved an audience from the time I was born. My mother and my father were my first audience, in a way. I behaved as I wanted them to think I behaved—but I didn't really behave that way at all. I had my own will and my own ideas.

When I look back over the landscape of my childhood, I believe that I was an odd child. It didn't appear at that time that I was odd at all. My interests were different from those of my sisters. They were more easy-going than I was, and I was more mannered than they were. I know that I was given certain privileges as an older child by my father and mother—mostly my father.

Geordie and Mary were able to get away with murder because if there was some upset about the house I was usually the cause of it. I was always the instigator of strange things that we did. Also, I usually took the blame because, with my dark mysterious looks, I appeared the most guilty.

One day, I decided that the doll house in the playroom was to be Little

Red Riding Hood's home. And so somehow we created village, forest, a path into the forest, and one that would lead Little Red out of the woods back toward the safety of home. Something, though, I believed was missing. I thought the toy fireplace would be much more alive with real fire and I placed a lit match inside. The smoke and flames were instant, and when Lizzie came running in and dashed a glass of water on it she said, "I know my little Geordie didn't do it, that girl is an angel." It was always Martha. Geordie got away with just about anything. When she was saying her prayers, or was supposed to, Lizzie would start her with "Now I lay me down to sleep," and instead of repeating it, Geordie would say, "All right." In other words, *You* say it; and we did, Lizzie and I. It was a wonderful life for Geordie to a point and then it became difficult. She could do so little for herself.

Perhaps it was the Red Riding Hood incident that convinced my parents to take me to a theatre—one outside of the upstairs playroom, and certainly out of the house. We were on holiday. We would go as a family to Atlantic City by horse-drawn carriage and stay in a hotel. The children ate in one area, the adults in another. My father always came to us in the children's dining room to see that we were eating exactly what he had ordered for us, and that we were listening to the nurse who sat with us. I found the idea of a hotel—to be in a house, separated from my own parents—a very odd thing.

I remember when a few of the children sat together under the boardwalk, in the cool shade. We could hear footsteps above us and see slats of sun through the wooden planks. Then we saw our nurse walking down to the water in her bathing suit and we were shocked! Adults were always very shocking when they were not fully dressed.

Here, in Atlantic City, my father would purchase Oriental porcelains. He was crazy about little Chinese things. Not just figurines, or bone-fragile ornaments, but practical pieces like a soup tureen, various trays and bowls we would use in our house. He became more and more enchanted by the

Lizzie holds William, and I sit between my sisters in the surf at Atlantic City, New Jersey.

Chinese and very interested in the East. My father gave me my first encounters with and love of the Orient.

Once, after lunch, he came and got Mary, Geordie, and me, and we walked on the Atlantic City boardwalk, which was, for me, a place of great amusements and confections. My father bought us each a Hokey Pokey ice cream. We continued walking until we arrived at a theatre. I was about six years old and this theatre was a Punch and Judy show. I was sitting on a green velvet pouf, one of those old-fashioned reclining chairs I could lean comfortably back on with my legs way out in front. I sat with other children in a semicircle and our parents were either standing behind us or sitting on tall chairs. When the curtain parted, there it was—another world, something to explore, delve into, make my own. There was a world created out of nothing, a world similar to yet of course very different from that which Lizzie had described. I thought, "Ah, there's a world, there's a world. I am going to find it!"

It was a frontier for me in that I could enter it completely, a frontier not as vast as the country to the west of us, or all that could and would later be explored in the heavens, but a frontier of the imagination—perhaps the most difficult landscape to cross. I was spellbound.

I had my own world. And my own world was the Lady of Shalott, things that I read, books, and the imagination they inspired. In my room, I had a little wooden chair with paintings of kittens on the back. I was so attached to that chair that I kept it for many years after I had outgrown it. When I would hear a word from my parents or Lizzie I'd return to my chair and say the word over and over until I got it right. I did not want to embarrass myself or disgrace my father by stumbling on it or mispronouncing it. This, I believe, is how I learned about the great appetite for life: bit by bit, word by word.

One Sunday, while my parents were on the West Coast, or at least somewhere between Pittsburgh and California, Lizzie took us to a building that was not a theatre, but a place of ceremony, mystery, and blessing— a Roman Catholic church. We walked into the building together as if entering a great hush, being let in on some important secret. I loved the lush, royal robes. I loved the formality, the ritual, and the discipline. I loved the almost incomprehensible message which seemed to permeate that area.

My father had been brought up a Roman Catholic until he was about nine or ten, which was the time of the Civil War. He and his parents moved from Hannibal, Missouri, where they were living, to the North because his grandfather was fighting in the Union Army. Though I've never told this before, we had slaves. They were never sold and always treated like one of the family. I am not proud of the fact that we had slaves, but in the mid 1800s in the South, that is the way that things were done.

One day, during the Civil War, members of the Confederate Army came for my great-grandfather because he was fighting on the other side. They wanted him badly, and they were greeted at the door by my great-grandmother, who stood there with her children and the slaves and her shotgun. She said: "Yes, gentlemen, you may enter, but the first man in dies."

She was a dead shot and would have killed for her family. At that

Lizzie, me, Aunt Re and her husband, Mary, Mother, Father, Geordie, and an Indian guide in Hot Springs, Arkansas.

time, a woman of the South had to learn to be a perfect shot because it was a time of great, sudden violence, and she would fear constantly for the safety of her family. I like to think that some of her blood flows through me still, though I have never needed to hold or shoot a gun.

In one of the first years of the twentieth century, I believe, we went on a holiday to Hot Springs, Arkansas, to visit some of my father's people. Uncle William, my father's brother, lived there, and his was a grand old house. What was most important on that trip was my presentation to the grande dame of the kitchen, who had been a slave. There was a great love for her in my father's family, and he, terrified I might display bad manners, coached me very carefully on how I should behave, what I was to say. I held my father's hand and was taken into the kitchen. She was a large woman, dressed completely in white, sitting in a rocking chair in the middle of the kitchen. Afternoon sunlight seemed to gather in her lap as I came forth to meet her. She held court here and was revered by all of us.

Years later, my company and I toured the South prior to the civil rights movement, and performed at Spelman College. I told the young women of the all-black college that I would see them at the evening performance. They said, "Oh, no, we can't go to the theatre. It is for whites only." I went directly to the impresario. It was his first sellout and I said, "I understand you have sold out for the night." "Yes," he replied, "for the first time." I said, "That is simply wonderful. I want twenty seats for tonight's performance." He asked why and I said, "For the students at Spelman College. Otherwise there will be no performance." "Impossible," he cried. And with that I told my crew and my dancers to pack up. There would be no show that night. The impresario panicked and changed his mind. Within a few minutes I had twenty seats for the women of Spelman College.

I feel that my father never quite drew away from the teachings of the Catholic Church. Dye your wool purple and you can never wash out that stain. Once I remember I did not want to go to Sunday school. It was beginning to bore me. My father came to my bedroom, stood on the pink Oriental rug he had purchased in Atlantic City and said, "You must go to Sunday school." I said, "I'm not interested in religion." He said, "I am not interested in your religion. You'll choose your religion when you grow up. But I am concerned with the fact that you will be a woman of the world who is able to choose her own religion."

Perhaps this is one of the reasons why it never took. To this day, I never ask people about their religion, whether it's politics—which is a religion—or sex, which is also a religion. That day, however, I went with the family to the church. With my sisters I went to the smaller room that housed the Sunday school.

In Pittsburgh, it was the Presbyterian Church that assumed authority over our lives, as it was my mother's and my grandmother's church—the Second United Presbyterian Church of Allegheny. To me it was a dark, rather sinister place, with just one little bunch of flowers on the pulpit. It seems to me now that it must have been the same aged and unfragrant arrangement that had stood on the pulpit for most of my early years. There was a minister who, each and every Sunday, gave a very long sermon and I would fidget in my seat. One Sunday the minister began to preach a sermon on infants in hell—fire, brimstone, the works—who had somehow fallen under the power of the devil. Father, who was a regular churchgoer, became very angry at the preacher. We were all together for a family gathering, and when the preacher started to describe the awful fate of these doomed babies, my father rose from his seat, pointed to the preacher, and said, "Sir, you are a liar." He got all his family out of the pew, and ushered us into the street.

I was confirmed a Presbyterian and attended the Presbyterian church, but the glamour, the glory, the pageantry, and the regality of which St. Augustine speaks was prevalent in the Catholic Church, not in the Presbyterian, which was so intellectual, so without the livingness of the body and the child-life that it became a kind of dread. One shining light was Mrs. Bellman, who during the service would leave her seat in the pew very near my family's, turn toward the congregation, and lead us in a song:

> *There were ninety and nine that lay safely*
> *in the shelter of the fold.*
> *But one was out on the hills*
> *far away from the gates of gold.*

I loved to sit very near to where she stood to sing. Her voice was filled with beauty and the divinity of care, which made the service possible for me. I still remember the little song all the children sang in church as the contributions were asked for:

> *Dropping, dropping, pennies*
> *From the sky above.*
> *They are all for Jesus,*
> *He will have them all.*

39

My first performance was in this church, though I must say it was rather unexpected, especially for my parents and grandparents. I heard the music from a song my father used to play (how often he would play and sing Gilbert and Sullivan to cheer himself up at home), and I began rocking on my mother's lap. I believe she had recently given birth to my sister Mary, and must have found my sudden movements rather uncomfortable. She placed me beside her on the pew, but shortly after, I emerged and started dancing down the aisle in my white dress. I don't think anybody had ever danced in this church before. The congregation was silent, except for the sudden gasp that came from my mother. She was absolutely scandalized.

At the time I was not very well behaved at all. I was stubborn and the only way my parents could get me to bed when it was still daylight, was to beckon me upstairs to Lilywhite's party. And as I drifted off to sleep on the white sheets and pillow, I realized that I had been had.

Throughout these early years of my life in Pittsburgh, I would listen to my father when he spoke to me, but would forget it completely if I wished. Though he believed in disciplining his children, he would not raise his voice when I was naughty. He would not hit me. Instead, he would simply say, "Oh Martha, you disappoint me so." Well, in a way that was worse, and when he spoke those few words it just about did me in.

40

Mary, Geordie, and me.

During one Christmas Eve my sisters and I were supposed to be asleep in our beds, but early Christmas Day, I sneaked into the nursery to discover all the wonderful presents wrapped with beautiful paper and tied with striped silk bows under the tree. We would go to the forest as a family to find a tree, and once we agreed on one, my father would cut it down, and at home, light the tree with candles. That morning he heard me and came in to find me where I was not supposed to be. He asked what I was doing. As if the tree and the gifts did not matter, I ran to the window and said, "Oh my heart is filled with joy at the sight of the beautiful falling snow."

I could see through the new snow, the reflection of my father's skeptical figure in the glass in front of me, his arms crossed, as he simply said, "Oh Martha . . ."

I continued to behave exactly as I wanted during these early years in Pittsburgh. In that sense I was a bad girl. I began to answer my father back a great deal. He liked that, actually. I believe he encouraged that quality, which he would have expected in a son. My father would say to me, "If you're going to make a scandal, Martha, make it a big one!"

My father began to treat me a little beyond my years. You see, he loved science and medicine. He loved beautiful women and he loved race horses. He was so handsome with his blond hair that he was called Goldie Graham. When I was still quite a child I was betting on horse races. I was too young to know what a race horse was or what a race track meant. He would put a dollar on a race horse—a trotter, I believe—and we would sit at the track and wait to see if we won. We'd watch the horses in good weather and bad weather—through the smooth turf and the splashing mud. I loved the sense of completeness, the sense of circle, how the animals in their athletic sleekness seemed to become the very essence of horse. I loved how we were granted the ability to choose our own excitement. It was a new frontier to be explored, a new kind of daringness. Sometimes our luck paid off, sometimes it did not. Either way, I learned to take my chances.

I think I was my father's favorite. He wanted a boy and I became the closest thing to it. Some years ago I was at a party with Charles Addams, the cartoonist. He complimented me on my work, and I complimented him on his. He then said to me, "Oh Martha, I'm a red-blooded American boy. Just like you!"

I was fourteen years old when my parents returned from one of their trips out West to say that they had found a home for us in California and that we would be moving to the town of Santa Barbara. Such a strange and exotic name compared to Pittsburgh. Here there was to be no coal, no afternoon darkness, no need to cover our faces in veils, and no veil of soot to cover our home. My parents were enamored of the West, especially my father, while I tried to imagine a life different from what I was used to—away from my bedroom, my neighborhood, the pond with the black

42

In Santa Barbara, a place of light and sun and air.

swan—away from the excitement and the diversity of Atlantic City.

We packed. Lizzie helped us gather all our things and place them in great trunks so that nothing would be lost, nothing broken. Grandmother of course was coming to live with us. Oddly enough, Father did not give up his practice in Pittsburgh. For as long as I can remember, he would travel across the country from California to Pennsylvania. How often he made these trips I cannot say.

There was only one train from Pittsburgh to California. We arrived at the station, tickets in hand, to begin our journey west. The trip across the country was very beautiful and very hot and it was to last for nine days. Our view out the window was changing constantly—the climate, the land, and, oh, the sky!

Grandmother, who was always very formal, was completely overdressed for the heat. Once, in one of the midwestern states, the train stopped and we were allowed to walk outside. Grandmother, who at home always sat upright in a tall wooden chair, hands clasped on her lap, now spread her skirt out on the green grass, and sat, exhausted from the heat. Perspiration dampened her high collar. I thought it was dreadful that she should sit on the ground and behave this way. Everything, it seemed, was changing.

I became ill. There was a porter who had a fondness for me and he used to carry me up and down the aisles of the train. For most of this trip I was sick and this wonderful porter carried me in his arms for a good deal of our nine days.

Farther out west we stopped in a rather empty town—such big lands we were being taken through, such immeasurable landscapes. It was a late afternoon sky, burning in its vividness in colors unknown to me before. In this particular town were tar pits and we walked as a family through footsteps of prehistoric animals. I remember these spaces in the earth to be enormous—my small foot being placed gently down in the memory of the foot of some ancestor to man, some animal becoming upright, the body learning to lift itself up and out of any prior history. Hands, the last part of the human body to evolve, unknown. We seemed so little that day.

Back on the train, I would go from one car to the next. Sometimes the porter would carry me, sometimes I'd go on my own. When I would stand at the end of the last car, the East was the home I was leaving, though of course now hundreds if not thousands of miles away. And when I'd run to the front car I'd watch the West unroll before me. It really was a frontier.

The heat and dust of it all—I don't know how we did it. But we did. There was one moment when we stopped somewhere in New Mexico. The Indians came to the train to trade, or just to look at us. I was stretching my legs, and a little girl no older than I stared at me until I realized it was the bunch of grapes I was holding and eating that she was looking at. She had never seen grapes, I thought, or perhaps she had, but had never tasted them. I knew that because I instinctively handed the grapes to her. I still cannot forget the image of her tasting what I am sure were her first grapes, very slowly and deliberately, until I think she forgot I was even there.

The train was taking us from our past, through the vehicle of the present, to our future. Tracks in front of me, how they gleamed whether we went straight ahead or through a newly carved-out mountain. It was these tracks that hugged the land, and became a living part of my memory. Parallel lines whose meaning was inexhaustible, whose purpose was infinite. This was, for me, the beginning of my ballet *Frontier*.

When we arrived in Santa Barbara we went straight to our new home that my parents had rented from Mrs. Alexander. It was yellow and absolutely charming. I remember being so excited by this new home I went to open all the drawers of the cupboard in the dining room to see what Mrs. Alexander had left for us to use. I counted every last domestic thing—fork, knife, and spoon.

Mother opened the windows and the sea breeze rushed in and suddenly the light gossamer curtains were flying in the wind, alive with the bright sunlight. I wanted to swallow that moment whole.

California was a world of flowers, Oriental people, people with Spanish blood, a life completely different from our life in Pittsburgh. It became a time of light and freedom and curiosity. I was thrilled with it.

My interest in the Orient came not only from the prettiness of the Chinese things in our home, but also by the fact that we were surrounded by Chinese people. They were very beautiful. They gave us gifts. They brought us fish to eat. Curiously, I have always felt more Asia than America.

The Chinese have a saying that I have always believed. "If you're sad or if you're angry or if you're depressed, you must not go on the street—emotions are a communicable disease." You will give it to someone else.

The Spanish and American communities never really mixed well in Santa Barbara. Many Spanish people prided themselves on the fact that a non-Spaniard had never entered their home. It was this lack of communication that caused a hilarious bit of trouble. It became time to name the

Frontier, *April 28, 1935.*

new hospital in Santa Barbara, and one city elder to the unending delight of the Spanish community picked a name from a Spanish list that "sounded just wonderful," with absolutely no desire to know its meaning. After all, it was just Spanish to them. The name was Sale Si Puedes—"Get Out If You Can."

The first time we walked out to a cliff in Santa Barbara, we were on high land that overlooked the blue, blue Pacific. We were at the edge of the country, overlooking what seemed to be the edge of the world. I became intoxicated with the light. Arms out wide I began to run and I began to fall, and it did not matter when I lost my balance. I kept running and falling down and picking myself up and saying, "It is so wonderful here." The sunlight was so rich, the landscape so clear, I drank in as much of it as my body could encompass.

Sometimes when I am in the studio today I think of the moment of movement; what the dancers are doing today, what I was doing then. I see what the body does when it breathes. When it breathes in, it is a release and when it breathes out, it is a contraction. You breathe in and you breathe out, in and out. It's the physical use of the body in action.

My technique is based on breathing. I have based everything that I have done on the pulsation of life, which is, to me, the pulsation of breath. Every time you breathe life in or expel it, it is a release or a contraction. It is that basic to the body. You are born with these two movements and you keep both until you die. But you begin to use them consciously so that they are beneficial to the dance dramatically. You must animate that energy within yourself. Energy is the thing that sustains the world and the universe. It animates the world and everything in it. I recognized early in my life that there was this kind of energy, some animating spark, or whatever you choose to call it. It can be Buddha, it can be anything, it can be everything. It begins with breath. I am sure that levitation is possible. I am not speaking mystically, I am speaking practically. I am sure that I could walk in the air, but my heart is not trained to stand the urgency of that flight, the movement that comes up through and rests against the heart.

From one bluff, we could see the ocean and the dolphins that called this particular area home. We had no breakwaters to take away their liberty. Oh, my first dolphin! A living creature urging itself out of the living sea. An arch of gray that was so beautiful to me, that particular curve and grace of the animal body. How it would leap into the air and down again. People could actually touch the dolphins and swim with them. I did not because they were too far away from where I stood to watch. They filled me with a special kind of excitement. They were beloved.

When I went down to the water, to the beach in the summer heat, I wore a bathing suit—though unlike any you would see on a beach today. I was covered up. I had pants on. They were a kind of bloomers, with a matching top of the same dark fabric. Yes, skin showed, but not in any kind of bizarre way. You covered up to be respectable in your bathing, and you never, ever would wear this costume anywhere else.

47

One of the first families we met as neighbors, and soon considered friends, was the Alfred Dreyfus family. Mr. Dreyfus had gone as far away as he could from France, where he had been condemned for treason. He took his whole family to settle in Santa Barbara, and he became a man who dealt in real estate. My sisters and I played with his children. When Mrs. Dreyfus and my mother had a formal tea, all the children would participate in our own tea ceremony. They became a very special family to us.

My friend Inez Harmer would come to my house and we would play dress-up. We had to make our own dramas because the only theatrical shows that came our way were fiestas, with great pampas grasses tied in the manes of the parading horses. Inez and I would spend hours pretending that we were ladies of the world.

During these early days in Santa Barbara we became affiliated with a Presbyterian church and as I got a bit older I began to teach in the Sunday school. Parents would bring young children to me in the downstairs of the church while they attended the upstairs service. I played the piano a little and sang. I didn't talk a great deal about religion because, frankly, I wasn't very interested in it. Upstairs, they were interested in it very, very much. They wanted to be good little Presbyterians. And of course, good little Presbyterians bored me to death.

I asked one little boy to whom I was teaching the Old Testament, "Where did they put Joseph?" He was also a little rebel and said, "Oh, they put him in a nutshell." This had nothing to do with Joseph, nothing to do with Pharaoh, nothing to do with what was happening upstairs. I will always remember his answer as he said what was unexpected, the thought that was in his mind.

Once, before the end of class, a sweet little six-year-old boy looked up at me and said, "Please, miss, may we have a story next week with damsels in it?" "Damsel" was a word in our lives that meant impossible things and beautiful things and *Let down my golden hair*. Who knows what damsels are? You believe in them in a way and in another way you know that they are fiction. I had four or five children at one time, and amused these children to the best of my abilities until the upstairs service was completed, and the children returned to their parents.

I began to take piano lessons at home, which was a time of great pleasure. A young man from town would come over at a specific time of day and spend perhaps an hour with me. I gave these music lessons all of my concentration, and did not, like many people I know, view practice as a chore. I would pick a piece of sheet music and bend it back and place it on the piano. Hands ready, I'd begin to play. On warm days, I'd keep the door to the garden open. When I first began to study the piano, my feet did not quite touch the floor.

There was a beautiful grove of oak trees that became a place for families to gather. One time, my family was gathered around a picnic table, for a Sunday afternoon lunch. Suddenly, without reason, except for what I was feeling in my body, I stood on the table and began to dance. There was no music playing, but still I felt movement. Mother, of course, when she turned around from her conversation with my aunt, was embarrassed and made me stop.

I got to know Lotte Lehmann, who was not much older than myself. She had this wonderful, wonderful voice. I remember going to a great lawned area where Lotte would sing. She had an audience of students and friends and would stand, dressed beautifully, in the mild wind. Lotte would put a piece of food in her mouth and wild birds would swoop down to eat. None of the birds ever touched her throat, which held the gift of her voice. They came for the food. We came to watch. I know this sounds out of the ordinary, which it was, but this is exactly what happened.

I think of birds as a beautiful part of animal life. They do you no harm if you do them no harm. Birds in my ballets are symbols of evil—they are so beautiful and so ominous. They are the chorus in *Night Journey*— no other animal can haunt you like a bird. You have moments you wish you couldn't remember but you do remember and you are a night journey. As your memory makes you relive your life when you are old, not when you are young, there are things you wish you had not done, but did.

Emily Dickinson said, "Hope is that thing with feathers that perches on the soul." It can be a vulture. There are good days when you have it and bad days when you don't. It is painful to remember too much.

Lizzie began to take my sisters and me to the Mission in Santa Barbara, which was called the Queen of the Missions. Founded by the Franciscan Fathers, it was the most beautiful of the Southern California Missions. I remember how the Sisters of St. Claire, devout followers of the ways of St. Francis, would lie prone in prayer in front of the altar. We were to be very quiet when this happened, though the quiet here was very different from that of the church I attended in Pittsburgh, or the Presbyterian church here in California. Something of the sunlight and the color of the stone permeated the service and gave it a kind of livingness.

The entire holiday season was a joy when we lived there, in a Catholic community, with the Jesuits. You celebrated the holidays with the lights and received and gave lovely presents. There was one Father who called on us every week. He never ate anything and never tried to convert us. He came to our house as a guest. I looked forward to his visits because he was so correct and so joyous. When I would see him downtown he would stop walking and I would stop walking and he'd make the holy sign of the cross, then we'd both proceed.

49

.   .   .

Once, we went with Lizzie to the lower part of California, to attend Mass. The Mass was spoken by a priest and two women who acted as acolytes. When the service ended the doors were flung open, and in the area outside of the church were Indians on horseback, firing shots into the air. This signified that we were now allowed to go into the area of the Indians. I remember still the darkness of the church and the ceremony and the moment of the open door, and the sudden entrance of new light. The Indian women were dressed in their costumes in a bower. They watched the men dance in a line.

Very near the church was a charred wooden stake and I was not encouraged to go near it, but I soon learned that it carried with it a story of ritual and murder. It seemed that an American woman came to this part of the country to teach. She had been given money by the government to teach the Indians, but when she ran out of funds and had no more to give, she was burned by the Indians. This I did not see, but I can still see that spent stake vividly in my mind.

When we returned another time there had been a death in a nearby pueblo. My sister Mary was walking with the Catholic priest, holding hands. Members of the pueblo leaned the wooden coffin against the door of the church, and an old lady dressed entirely in black sang mournfully, "Holy, Holy Son."

I was as willful as ever in Santa Barbara and, as the eldest, was given certain chores to keep me in line, just as in Pittsburgh. It was my job to go into the garden with a bucket and remove the snails from the calla lilies.

We had night-blooming cereus, a plant like the fragrant jasmine, in the garden at the back of the house. It was Mother's delight. Mary, Geordie, and I would go out late in the evening to look for the flowers, which bloomed only in the moonlight. We were barefoot in our bedclothes, and carried shaded candles in our hands—any stronger light and the blossoms would close.

I'd breathe in the garden and as we hunched over the plant I'd notice the beautiful faces of my two sisters—their facial bones, their very eyes. Mary was the beauty. She had blond hair and blue eyes and, even as a child, long, long legs. When Mary was a bit older and went to Chinatown in San Francisco, my parents feared terribly that she would be kidnapped and sold into white slavery. This was not an unusual occurrence, and with Mary's looks, my parents had all the more reason to fear. One time, when Mary was wearing her beautiful green coat on the train, a man followed her off into Santa Barbara because he was looking for a wife, and Mary fit the bill.

Geordie, too, was very pretty, with dark, curly hair and large brown eyes. I was part wild and part civilized. I had a long face and straight hair and I was very thin—not what would be called an attractive child. I felt that not having either blond hair or curly hair made me, in some way, an outsider.

Mary, Mother, me, and Geordie in Santa Barbara.

. . .

The blossoms of the cereus were a delicate white filled with the mystery of life and the fact that they only lived at night. Fragrant and flamboyant, not understandable. This made upon me a direct and terrific mark. I said that sometime I would have a dress, a costume for the stage modeled on the inspiration of those nights and that flower. And I did. The dress was that of the Virgin, in white, in *Primitive Mysteries*, my 1931 ballet. It was a kind of organza which had an energy, a life, and an envelopment as if it were a cloud.

The evening before the first performance of *Primitive Mysteries* the dance was not working. I told the dancers to go home, that it would not appear on the next day's program. I felt that it was a failure and locked myself in my dressing room for three hours. It is then that composer Louis Horst, my musical director, defied me. "Louis," I said, "you are breaking me. You are breaking my very soul." He told the girls to stay. He told me, "You must

53

Primitive Mysteries, *February 2, 1931.*

come out and be seen and do this. We will work it out." The next evening, *Primitive Mysteries* was the last piece on the concert program. Groups of women in dark, long dresses entered. I entered in my white organdy dress. This was the Hymn to the Virgin, then Hosanna and Crucifixus. We moved at first to an absence of music. Then it was Louis's music. We were enveloped.

My father, with another doctor, owned an olive ranch in Montecito, a town south of Santa Barbara. To get there, Grandmother would drive us over in a carriage pulled by horses, though we had an automobile.

There was an olive branch quite high off the ground. It must have been six or seven feet high and it was to this branch that I climbed with my skipping rope in hand. It was a stunning day and my climb seemed to take me closer to the source of the heat and the light. I stood tall. I began to skip rope slowly, then I quickened my pace.

My mother had watched me from the house and ran to the tree where I was. She stood absolutely still, petrified that if she spoke to me I would stop and fall down. I did not. I was too intent on moving. When I stopped, I dropped the rope and left the tree on my own. However, I was never permitted outside of the house alone with a rope to climb the tree and indulge in the wildness of skipping. My mother always feared my next move—and for good reason—as her expression revealed in so many of our photographs.

For a time I sat under the shade of an olive tree. I pulled on a branch of olives and let the precious oil run over my hands and my arms and I brought some of it to my tongue. It seeped through my clothes—it even seemed to have the ability to penetrate my skin. Though my body had quieted from the motion of skipping rope, something deeper was going through me at the time. I still remember that day in the sunlight and how the olive oil heightened and stained my skin.

In Santa Barbara.

We had a go-cart on the ranch which was terribly exciting. We were driven by a donkey that pulled the weight of the wooden cart. Mary was usually terrified by the ride and especially the animal, but I'd encourage the donkey to quicken by stroking its back. This terrified Mary even more.

One day I was walking with my parents down the Main Street of town, away from the Mission and toward the Pacific. In one of the stores there was a poster advertising a dance performance by Miss Ruth St. Denis. This, I believe, was in 1911, and Miss Ruth, as I would later call her, had just completed successful performances in San Francisco. She was touring up and down the coast of California and would be appearing in Los Angeles shortly. She was a woman with a great shock of long white hair, costumed in something reminiscent of the Orient. This image not only caught my eye and my imagination, it became my obsession.

Though my parents continued to walk toward the beach, I called them back and showed them the poster. I begged them to take me to Los Angeles, and after a bit of time, my father agreed, though Mother never ever liked the place. She would have nothing to do with Los Angeles.

When the day of the dance performance came my father and I traveled to Los Angeles, not by automobile and not by horse-drawn carriage. We traveled by ferry, which left from Santa Barbara and stopped in many small towns along the coast before arriving in the large city that was our destination.

I went to the theatre, the Mason Opera House, with a dark dress and hat that my father had bought for me. It was matronly in design and detail, more for a fifty-year-old woman, but that is what he knew. I thought I was dressed very elegantly, but evidently I was dressed well beyond my years. He pinned a corsage of violets to my gray dress and that night my fate was sealed. The curtain parted. The audience was still. Miss Ruth was doing a program that included her famous solos—"The Cobras," "Radha," and "Nautch." Also on the program was her famous dance "Egypta."

I became so enamored of Ruth St. Denis as a performer; she was more than exotic—I realize now she was a goddess figure. I knew at that moment I was going to be a dancer. I learned she was a farm girl from New Jersey who as a child used to sell watercress she picked herself on a farm called Pin Oaks. This money enabled her mother to encourage her daughter's dancing through the various trips and auditions that awaited her in New York City. I decided at that moment I would dance and when I learned she had a school I made up my mind to attend it. But I still had my classes to go to at Santa Barbara High School. Despite what people have said

High school graduation.

about me and my upbringing, my parents never objected to my becoming a dancer. They didn't say, *No, you won't become a dancer.* They never interrupted me. I could do anything I wanted. I found myself inclined that way—the inclination to be beautiful and wild, maybe a creature of another world. I always have been myself in that sense. When I was wild I was wild. When I was a lady later in years, I tried to be a lady. In each character I played, I played according to what I felt was the wild one.

It wasn't as though I had violated any laws of the family by dancing. I used to walk around barefoot and I would sit with my mother on the porch. She became very excited about my wanting to be a dancer and liked to look at my bare feet.

Some time after this, I ran into the Presbyterian minister on the train in Santa Barbara. He came and sat with me and said, "Now I hope you've really made up your mind to be a teacher of children. You're wonderful." I said, "Oh no, I am going to be a dancer." He stood up, turned his back on me, and walked away. And that was that. He never spoke to me again.

In high school I studied English literature. One day, out of the blue, Mr. Olney, the principal, took over our English class for a session. We were reading quietly to ourselves, when suddenly Mr. Olney announced that he would like to call Martha Graham to the front of the class to read from the *Idylls of the King* by Alfred, Lord Tennyson. I was shocked.

I took my place at the front of the room and began to read aloud the heroic story of King Arthur and the Knights of the Round Table. You have to remember that the first part of this poem appeared only thirty-five years before my birth. The poem begins with the poet's dedication to Prince Albert, who was a great admirer of the *Idylls* but who died a year before their publication. And so I recited:

"These to His Memory—since he held them dear,
Perchance as finding there unconsciously
Some image of himself—I dedicate,
I dedicate, I consecrate with tears—
These Idylls."

I was spellbound by the unfurling of the tale, and so was the class—
and I might add Mr. Olney as well. In a way I became one of the idylls.
I was thrown into it, but not devoured by it. It was a story and I was the
storyteller.

In high school I also played on the school's basketball team. All the
women on the team wore the same brown uniform. I wore my long hair
in a single braid that swung across my back as I ran across the gymnasium
floor in an attempt to make a hoop. I believe I took quite naturally to this
sport because I wanted to move. Many of my girlfriends at this time knew
how to dance, but not me. I think this is one of the reasons I took up
basketball in the first place.

I was editor-in-chief of the high school yearbook, *The Olive and Gold.*
Under my small oval photograph was the following:

> *Capable, generous, willing to do—*
> *To the noblest standards, faithful and true.*

The school play that year was *Prunella* by Laurence Houseman and
Granville Barker. I played Privacy, the timid yet loving aunt. *The Olive
and Gold* reprinted the following review from the *Morning Press,* April 6,
1913:

> The interpretation of "Privacy," the aunt who remains in the forlorn
> garden waiting for Prunella's return, was a fine bit of acting. Miss

Martha Graham's voice exactly suited the part and she was careful not to overact when she discovered that the man who had bought her house is he who lured Prunella away. Sincerity and artistic appreciation of proportion marked every moment of Miss Graham's admirable work.

Looking back, I can sense how wretched I must have been.

Suddenly, our whole world shifted. My father died while with us in California. This was the great tragedy that marked my teens, my childhood. I thought of William again, my young brother who died as an infant. Everything again seemed as dark as Pittsburgh. We were left a house of women—mother, Lizzie, Geordie, Mary, and myself.

A few years after he died the money disappeared. Mother had to move into a less expensive house and take in boarders. It was a very bitter time. The minute my father died, the man with whom he owned the ranch in Montecito sold it to another corrupt man. He embezzled the funds and we had no more money.

Five years after going with my father to see Ruth St. Denis I appeared in Los Angeles for my first summer course. I had already attended the Cumnock School of Expression after high school where literature, art, and dramatics were very much the curriculum. It was, however, nothing at all like Denishawn.

The Denishawn school was located about ten minutes from the heart of the Los Angeles business district. We were isolated from that, on top of a hill, surrounded by tall and fragrant eucalyptus trees. I still have the program from my first session, the second summer of the school, when we were on St. Paul Street. The brochure said, "The unique offering of Denishawn is the dance as a finished product, complete with orchestrated music, costume, lighting effects, properties, and scenery."

At first I was taken into a room that was filled with green curtains. There was a large man at the piano smoking a cigar who said nothing to

Seated second from left with the students and teacher of the Cumnock School of Expression, 1916.

me. I waited and then suddenly Ruth St. Denis appeared. She said, "Dance for me." I said, "Miss St. Denis, I have never danced before and don't know anything about it." "You must know how to do something," she said. "No, I don't." She turned to the man at the piano, whom she called Louis, and instructed him to play something, anything, a waltz. I don't recall how I reacted beat by beat to the music but I moved, I moved furiously. I danced. I don't think she was very impressed by my interpretation of the music, and when Louis stopped playing, she put me in her husband Ted Shawn's care.

Some of the classes in the Denishawn curriculum were dramatic gesture—based on the system of François Delsarte; plastique movements—learning the decorative use of the body and the study of body line; and piano lessons by Louis Horst, musical director. We also had ballet classes under Miss Edson, who was a holy terror. At the time I started in ballet

Ruth St. Denis.

they were dancing "The Spirit of Champagne" on pointe, in Paris. I thought, "I don't want to dance the spirit of champagne, I want to drink it!"

There was also a Denishawn Red Cross auxiliary where the girls learned to "do their bit." We had lessons in craft work—designing and making costumes, jewelry, properties, and decorative background.

Miss Ruth and Ted staged a dance pageant of Egypt, Greece, and India, for the school as well as for students at the University of California. It was held on the Berkeley campus, at the famous Greek theatre, built by William Randolph Hearst. It seemed as if there were a countless number of dancers on the stage with an infinite number of costumes and costume changes. I appeared in the first part of the pageant, "Egypt," as one of the Dancers with Triangles.

Ruth St. Denis was a goddess figure and a deeply religious being, but she was also a performer. Once, when we were watching her in an East Indian ballet, she dropped a rose. We thought it was an accident, but it was deliberate. The fact that she decided to drop the rose at that point . . . well, I was utterly beguiled by it. It was completely planned. I learned that it is the planning of those little things that sometimes makes the magic, the real magic.

63

Miss Ruth had a great love of the body, of beauty, and a knowledge of things not generally known in the dance world, which at the time was Isadora Duncan, whom I never saw, and ballet. I had very strict training at the Denishawn school.

Denishawn was a school of the arts. Every afternoon, Miss Ruth, in a luminous sari, would read to us from Mary Baker Eddy and the *Christian Science Monitor*. She would usually stroke her favorite pet, an exquisite peacock called Piadormor, while intoning his name to him over and over. It was like a litany—it calmed him. The students sat on the small bridge that linked two ponds, which were filled with carp and lotus blossoms. Piadormor would

With Piadormor, Miss Ruth's exquisite peacock.

At twenty-two, my Denishawn debut as Priestess of Isis in a pageant staged by Ted Shawn and Miss Ruth.

let me pick him up, and when I spoke to him, he would open his exquisite feathers.

Miss Ruth would read to us from her own poetry as well. I will always remember the following poem, which Miss Ruth chose to be inscribed on her tombstone:

The Gods have meant
That I should dance
And in some mystic hour
I shall move to unheard rhythms
Of the cosmic orchestra of heaven,
And you will know the language
Of my wordless poems
And will come to me,
For that is why I dance.

Other times Miss Ruth dressed in a beautiful Japanese kimono with a band around her head. She would talk gibberish to us and we would talk gibberish to her. In other words, we were creating our own area of something Japanese, our own vocabulary. We were learning to improvise. She and Ted Shawn had a theatre built for themselves where many Orientals, the residents of Los Angeles, came to watch the performances.

Miss Ruth wanted Denishawn to embody the spirit of America and to fit the American need much better than any foreign system. While Denishawn used foreign techniques, we were not restrained by them when necessity called for individuality.

Because my odd dark looks made me appear somewhat Oriental, Miss Ruth tried to pass me off as a Japanese boy. I had been helping Miss Ruth in a dance that revolved around the Japanese art of flower arranging. She liked this and decided I would be billed as a Denishawn discovery—an Oriental boy. I was not a child at this time and Miss Ruth had plans to bind me up. I said to her, "But Miss Ruth, I will have breasts and then what will I do?" She did not answer. When my mother got wind of this she put her foot down and absolutely forbade it. She said to Miss Ruth, "Martha does not resemble a Japanese boy!"

Miss Ruth's mother would often come to Los Angeles to be with her daughter. I was not dancing then and it was assumed that my time was free, so Miss Ruth assigned me to tend to her mother, who was a bit addled, during meals. Miss Ruth's mother was always very well dressed, but when she appeared for breakfast, lunch, or dinner, she had fifteen safety pins attached to the left side of her suit. She would cut her food carefully, and after taking a bite and taking the time to chew slowly, she would move one of the safety pins to the right. It was my job to make sure none of the pins fell into her food because Miss Ruth worried that she might not find the pin before the next bite. Three times a day!

Sometimes Miss Ruth would call me into her room to help her wash her hair, which was beautiful—long and white. I didn't mind this. It was an honor for me to have anything to do with Miss Ruth.

At Denishawn we slowly became involved in the mythologies of other peoples. I remember being dressed often in Burmese costumes—a skirt which was very thin and very Oriental, a little white jacket and sandals.

When I first came to Denishawn I was teaching children. They did not think I would ever perform because I wasn't beautiful. I was not blond and I did not have curly hair. These were the Denishawn ideals. At twenty-two they thought I was good enough to be a teacher, but not a dancer. They saw nothing of a performer in me. But since I photographed well and had impact, they used a picture of me as a temple dancer in their brochure.

Miss Ruth had her own room which was green and had many green curtains. We all lived together in the Denishawn house. Even though I was not allowed to dance, I secretly did. One night I went quietly down

Photographed with impact for the Denishawn brochure.

the steps from my room to Miss Ruth's studio. It must have been around two o'clock in the morning because it was pitch dark and the house was completely still. I was in the darkness, dancing and practicing alone. Charles Weidman, who would come to partner me here and at the Neighborhood Playhouse in New York, and would found his own company with Doris Humphrey, reminded me of this years later. He came downstairs and found me dancing but he said nothing then. I was doing my own movements, trying to find strange, beautiful movements of my own. I would dance and rehearse in absolute darkness until dawn. When the time came for me to dance I would be ready.

. . . .

68

With Charles Weidman at Denishawn.

I was afraid that I would be sent away from Denishawn. I never felt that they believed in me. I worshiped everything about Miss Ruth—how she walked, how she danced. Miss Ruth was everything to me, but I got stuck with Ted, who really was something of a dud.

Ted Shawn had choreographed a solo called *Serenata Morisca*, a Moorish dance, and I was allowed to teach it in four lessons at the school. One day he was trying to decide which dancers would perform this on the road. The lead dancer had fallen ill. He looked over the dancers on the platform, then over to where I was sitting. "It's too bad Martha doesn't know a dance. If she did she might replace her." I stood up to him and said that I could dance *Serenata Morisca*. He said, "Really, Martha? You've never danced. You've never studied with me. How can you do it?" I got up quickly, hastily put on a skirt, and did *Serenata Morisca*. I went up to him afterward and said a bit breathlessly, "Was it so terrible?" He said, "No, that is always how I wanted it to be performed. It was completely professional. And you'll do it in San Diego." I was called to do it at a gala at the submarine base in San Diego. I think it was the fact that I decided I could do it and just did it that shocked Ted. It alarmed and amazed him so much that he allowed me to do it.

It was the beginning of my career, and became one of the ballets I performed in the *Greenwich Village Follies*. Doris Humphrey and I both danced it in Denishawn; it was the only ballet we shared. When Doris did *Serenata Morisca* she exited stage left, on a diagonal. When I performed it, I spun in a nautch turn, to the floor, center stage. It's a harder way to end and to hold the audience. I was so arrogant that I didn't give it a second thought. I just did it.

Doris and I had completely different views of choreography, a word I never heard of until I reached New York. At Denishawn, you just made up dances. Doris felt that everything could be taught according to rules and diagrams. I had always felt it was a far deeper, more visceral thing. I suppose we were rivals in a way. It reached a point where Doris called me "some exotic hothouse flower" or more directly, "that snake." I always hoped she meant a cobra. I really did not take that much notice of her with the exception of wanting to be the seamless choreographer she was. For, at Denishawn, Martha was the one who danced, and Doris was the one who made up dances.

Doris's book *The Art of Making Dances* became a great success and I was glad for her, but a little put off with some of its concepts. The chapter that just did me in was entitled "The Center of the Stage." To Doris, it was a geographic place in the middle of things. When I saw it I thought, "But the center of the stage is where I am." Doris did, however, light up the center of the stage, wherever it was, as very few artists did.

. . .

Ted became quite fond of me and confided certain things to me. He had once been a Methodist divinity student and had started out ballroom dancing during afternoon teas. Ted liked to surround himself with the company of men, and had beautiful male dancers in his company and at Denishawn. Whenever Ted had a fight with a boyfriend—and he did have boyfriends though he and Miss Ruth were utterly devoted to each other—he'd sulk. The rehearsal would come to a halt. It was up to me to comfort him.

"Oh Ted," I'd say, "don't worry about him. He doesn't understand you and does not have the right to say what he said to you." Ted was so beside himself, so distraught, that it was up to me again to console him. "Ted," I'd tell him, "you are much too good for him. It is best if he goes." And this comforted him for a time until it happened again. I hated to do this, but I wanted to stay at Denishawn. I only wanted to dance.

Ted had his own way of auditioning the men for Denishawn. They had to send nude pictures of themselves, and God knows what else, which came from all different areas of the country. I thought it was rather horrible. I'd never seen anything like it before in Santa Barbara.

Ted was vain, and was beguiled by the idea of displaying himself in nude photographs and in dance. Later, when he went with Miss Ruth and the Denishawn company to Asia, with my sisters and Doris Humphrey, they visited the Kabuki, which for a person in the dance or in the theatre was akin to a shrine. Each of the various artists, Miss Ruth down to the newest member of the company, was allowed to walk the elegant path to the hanamichi, the entrance of the gods. All except Ted, that is. They had seen him dance and felt that as an artist, he was impure. That was the difference between Ted and Miss Ruth. Miss Ruth was a goddess when she danced. Ted was a dancer dressed as a god.

I had learned that the hanamichi came from the days when the Kabuki and the No were first performed in dry riverbeds. To me it represented

70

MARTHA GRAHAM

A delightful study of Martha Graham, a student of Ruth St. Denis
and Ted Shawn at their Denishawn School. Miss Graham is
shown in an authentic Oriental costume for one of her
charming renditions

Serenata Morisca, *1917. Finally, I was allowed to dance.*

the river of life, the change, the rush that carries you forward. Heraclitus said it when he stated, "You can never place your foot in the same river twice."

One time, after participating in a performance at the school, I went into the kitchen and heard one of the teachers say to Ted, "Martha is the best dancer you will ever have. Treasure her and take care of her." I was so frightened and so scared that I left the kitchen because I did not know what was coming next.

There was a time when Ted was choreographing a new dance and he wanted to use Miss Ruth in it but she said, "No, I am too old and I cannot do it." Ted said, "Well, it's too bad that Martha's a virgin and cannot do this dance." This made me absolutely furious and I said, "Mr. Shawn, you don't mean to say that you think I am a virgin." "Now Martha," he said, "we must not jest about sacred things." This made me even angrier.

Miss Ruth was a deeply spiritual being. Once when we were alone, she said, "Martha, I am going to share a bit of the Bible with you that a very old woman gave to me when I was a young girl like you." This was Habakkuk, the last few lines: "The Lord God is my strength, and he will make my feet like hinds' feet, and he will make me to walk upon mine high places. To the chief singer on my stringed instruments." I have repeated these lines to myself so many times for comfort and to others as well.

One time when I danced in Israel in a Jewish piece, I was the only non-Jew. When I suddenly made a point and then added, "But I am only a shiksa," they all laughed an embarrassed laugh. I said, "But isn't that what you call me in private?" "Well, I've seen everything," somebody replied, "I've seen a girl call herself a shiksa and at the same time quote the Old Testament."

When I danced *Baal Shem* to the music of Ernest Bloch, a woman, very Gentile, came backstage to congratulate me on my use of sacred Jewish writings. She looked at me and said, "Miss Graham, you identified so totally with the Jewish heroine. I realized that you as a Jewess would identify with one of your own race more than one of us." I said, "I am very honored, but I am not Jewish." Well, she clearly didn't believe me as I thanked her for the compliment. She turned to leave, took my arm and at the door said to me, "My dear, never deny your heritage."

You see, I believe so completely in the life of a human being and the sanctity of a human being. I do not care about what the nationality is. I have this terrific appetite for life and the experience of what life means.

Baal Shem, *November 28, 1926.*

It does not matter if you are in Timbuktu, or wherever. You stand and you are an individual and you are beautiful. That, to me, is very sacred.

I met Louis Horst, this huge, great spirited musician and composer, at Denishawn. He would become a major influence in my life. His father was a musician, too, and played in the orchestra pit. The first time Louis's mother took him to see a dance, they were sitting in the balcony and Louis called down to his father in very loud terms, "Papa, beer, beer!"

Louis had come to Denishawn to take the place of Miss Ruth's accompanist for approximately ten days or so. He stayed ten years. Once we were doing something called musical variations, and I passed the piano where Louis was, the piano I still have, while he played music from the *Unfinished Symphony*. I was supposed to be an oboe because I had a deep tone and seemed melancholy. Louis said, "You are off the beat with that oboe. Get into it more clearly and relate yourself to the sound of the oboe!" and put me in my place. I was very upset. Whenever Louis disapproved of anything, we dancers all took it very seriously. He was a great man in the sense that he believed the dance to be more than the music or the dance, but really, life itself. He encouraged all the different dancers to be their best. He felt the dance was music; that which you expressed through the dance was the figure of music. The identity with music and dance was, I think, the theme of his life. He would not tolerate mediocrity. When it came, he would smash it. He believed in the dance and in the fact that I had something curious and wonderful to give which I was not aware of at all.

He would give an edge to a dancer—the best criticism but the worst thing to hear. If what I did did not please him, because he thought I could do better, he'd say, "It's not good enough. Stop it. Begin again." "But, Louis, you're breaking me. You're killing my soul!" I'd say. "Begin again," he'd say. "But you're killing my soul," I'd cry again and finally Louis would dismiss me with "Then let it die now," and he'd turn from me with disdain.

Louis felt that music for the dance should not overwhelm or in any way overshadow the dance movement. He did not want me to use strings in any of the compositions I would later commission for my dances. He preferred piano, percussion, and wind instruments. He did not want strings in any of the music because he felt they were too lush and too romantic— in other words, deadly to contemporary dance.

Your body does not feel the same when you dance to strings as when you dance to woodwinds. It simply cannot. It doesn't even feel the same when you dance to a flute or a bassoon. There is a different thing which hits against your body. The wall of sound holds you in a certain way. You rest on that tone.

Louis had a wonderful sense of life about himself and a keenness of humor. He made up names for us: I became Mirthless Martha; Doris Humphrey was Doric Humphrey, because she was always doing Greek dances. Later, when we moved to New York, Agnes de Mille became Agony Agnes because he felt Agnes had a tendency to collect grievances and play a martyr at times. He called Helen Tamiris Tam Tam Tamiris because she did a ballet he disapproved of—more like a strip tease he said, particularly when she exited stage right and dropped her only semblance of decency, a silk scarf. Louis was furious.

Louis lived across the street from me in New York. He had a museum-quality collection of kachina dolls and many American things, although he himself was not what he called an American; he had rather European ways, but he became an American. He indulged himself in it and he insisted upon us being Americans. Louis knew the Southwest. He took me there. I felt much of the Indian through him because he felt so deeply the passion, the great things the Indian has to offer us. That's why I never learned any European dances. Nothing of that kind entered his mind. He insisted that we be of the time we were in, of the place we were in, which was

America. He was, I think, one of the great American artists of the age.

These days in Los Angeles were very difficult. I had one good dress made of pleated white silk, a bit like a Fortuny, but on my salary, not the real thing. Each evening before going to bed, I would wash it and hang it to dry. In the morning I would iron it. It didn't bother me, and I had more to worry about than my lack of dresses.

I wore this dress when I was sent to audition for Cecil B. DeMille's film *Male and Female*. When I arrived, I changed into a Babylonian priestess costume—a heavy jet-beaded bra and tight dress with a bare midriff. I wore heavy eye makeup and a great, curling wig.

The sound stage was an unsettling sight. In a far corner was a beautiful young woman, the nineteen-year-old Gloria Swanson, reclining on a chaise longue while she read her script. Lions roamed all around her. I was terrified! One padded right by me as if sleepwalking, then fell over sideways like a cardboard cutout, but with a tremendous thud. I walked by these half-awake animals and realized they were drugged and harmless. After my audition for Mr. DeMille, I wished I had been drugged, too.

Mr. DeMille sat at the end of a fifteen-foot red carpet. He wore a typical director's costume, everything down to a riding crop and a megaphone. At his side stood a slightly trembling secretary who held a clipboard. Mr. DeMille said nothing to me, but shouted out his directions to his secretary. He would not address me directly, although I could hear every word he said.

"Tell her to turn around." And his secretary would repeat to me, "Mr. DeMille would like you to turn around." I turned.

"Tell her to fall down." I fell.

"Tell her to do a dance step." I did a dance step.

I got the part, but to this day I don't know if the dancing girl in the dream sequence of the film is me.

Many years later, Paramount Pictures would offer me a large sum to release the rights to the Martha Graham story. They wanted Cyd Charisse to play me, and Tony Martin to play Louis Horst. Of course, funding in the arts is difficult, and it takes a lot to run a company and a school and we were in need, but tempted as I was I said, "No, absolutely not. I can ruin my own reputation in five minutes. I don't need help."

Ted Shawn was choreographing a piece about an Indian princess on me, based on his studies of the Mayan, Aztec, and Toltec cultures. He chose me to dance the title role of Xochitl.

Ted would play the role of Emperor Tepancaltzin, who would later try to rape me. It was an opulent production, with Ted wearing an extraordinary headdress of feathers and flowers. I believe Ted chose me because he felt that I had some crazy ideas in me and that I could be a girl like Xochitl, "the flower." Xochitl was the most beautiful of all the chaste Toltec maidens, whose father produced an intoxicating wine from the flowers of the maguey plant. When Xochitl's father brought the wine to the king with his daughter in tow, the king drank and asked the mysterious Xochitl to dance. And then he proceeded to make his advances . . .

I remember how repetitively Ted would choreograph this piece. He kept going over and over and over the same thing, but never quite lighting on what it was he wanted, until I finally said, "Mr. Shawn, if perhaps you just told us what you want, we'll do it."

Nobody had really talked to him like this before.

Miss Ruth, when she heard me speak up, came to me and said, "Martha, you'll be very good for Teddy."

There's a part in *Xochitl* when I lean way back in order to display myself to the king. This was the rape scene. It was the only time that I saw that I was being chased by the king. I was the prettiest girl—they thought—and I used fans as part of his enticement. I carried a bowl of wine. He chased me around the stage and he was very big and strong and

made me so angry. It was a rape scene, or an attempted rape scene, and I tried to focus all of my energy into this thought of anger and violation, although I knew that with Ted, I was as safe as in the arms of Jesus.

But he gave a convincing portrayal all right—too convincing. At one point he grabbed me and dropped me on my head and I passed out for a few seconds. When I came to I bit him on his arm and drew blood. After I did that he ran from one side of the stage to the other, front and back, dripping blood. And it became a great *scandale* in the school. I suppose that is when my reputation for having a violent temper began.

I was savage at that time. The critics said that onstage I blazed, and that is still my favorite review after all these years. I would do anything to be onstage. Theatre was a wonderful world. I did every section completely as Ted choreographed it. I was almost like an animal in my movements. I wanted to be a wild, beautiful creature, maybe of another world—but very, very wild.

Xochitl had its premiere in Long Beach, California, in June 1920. Later that year I would be back home in Santa Barbara and interviewed by the *Santa Barbara News:*

"So far the only value of my work—if it has art value—is absolute sincerity. I would not do anything that I could not feel. A dance must dominate me completely, until I lose sense of anything else. Later what I may do may be called art, but not yet."

Louise Brooks was a member of the Denishawn company and breathtakingly beautiful. She wore her hair always in that pageboy. Everything that she did was beautiful. I was utterly absorbed by her beauty and what she did. Even before she was introduced to me, I remember watching her across the room as she stood with a group of girls from Denishawn, all dressed alike. Louise, though, was the absolute standout, the *one*. She

Xochitl, *June 1920.*

With Robert Gorham in Xochitl, *1921.*

possessed a quality of strength, an inner power that one felt immediately in her presence. She was very much a loner and terribly self-destructive. Of course, it didn't help that everyone gave her such a difficult time. I

Dancing outdoors with Ted Shawn in Malagueña, *1921.*

suppose I identified with her as an outsider. I befriended her, and she always seemed to be watching me perform, watching me in the dressing room. She later said, "I learned how to act by watching Martha Graham dance."

Louise was quite young, sixteen or so, and had a habit of wearing a very tight pair of shoes. Well, this made me angry, and before we were to go on the stage one evening for a performance, I grabbed her, shook her, and yelled at her that she was going to ruin her feet with those tight shoes.

I remember one time with Louise in the wings when we received a phone call from Ted Shawn. We were on the road, on the circuit, without him, and he was calling to tell us that our work was unsatisfactory. He wanted us to return home to Los Angeles. I don't know who received the call and was relaying his message to the rest of us. All I know is that this particular phone was the old-fashioned kind you had to crank. I said, "The hell with you, I will not be talked to that way."

I got up from my chair, went to the wall, pulled the telephone right off the wall, and threw it onstage. I think that Louise and the rest of the dancers were stunned, but when called upon, my temper was ready. I was a heller! I was capable of great violence, which those around me called my "black Irish rages." I had a very bad temper, very bad. I still have it though I do not use it often. I've learned not to allow myself to indulge in it. But I can use it, if need be, on occasion.

Once, Louise and I were backstage preparing to go on, and I was pinning flowers into my hair, arranging the bottles of makeup that were in front of me, deciding which creams to apply. We had our own Denishawn body cream that we used to cover our skin, and since it was specially made for us, we had to carry around our own bottles on tour. Louise was on my right in the dressing room, and a few other girls were there as well.

I cannot say for certain what I was thinking of, but some anger seized me—and I took one of the bottles and smashed it against the mirror, which shattered into a thousand pieces. I said nothing. Louise said nothing. I simply gathered my belongings and moved to another mirror. I happily applied my makeup; we went onstage.

There were times when Lizzie and my mother would come down to Los Angeles to visit us. Once, they were staying with me in my room at Denishawn, when we were suddenly woken by the most awful screams coming from the house next door. We looked at each other in the night as the sound of something crashed. Lizzie turned to my mother and said, "Murder is going to be laid out in that room." Needless to say, in the morning we were very curious to see who would emerge from that house.

On tour with Denishawn: Ted and Miss Ruth at the top of the stairs; I'm to her right.
Louise Brooks is in the center, wearing a hat with four white stripes. Louis Horst is to her left.
Robert Gorham and Charles Weidman are seated in front.

For a time, Lizzie stood by the window, but there was no telling what had gone on next door.

Although I was dancing with the troupe, it was my job to accompany Miss Ruth to church services on Sunday when we were touring the states. Whether it was Kansas or Ohio or wherever, Miss Ruth always scouted out the church, and somehow, come Sunday morning, I would be sitting next to her on a wooden pew, my back straight, my thoughts somewhere between the present time and the memories of the Presbyterian services of my childhood. Both had the ability to keep me upright in my seat. I wonder what the local people thought of Miss Ruth and me, two odd-looking women, without any sign of chaperons.

One Sunday, I recall, was completely dreary. We were in a small town, and it was raining, and the sky seemed to be bathing us not only in water but in the color gray as well. The service was, to put it mildly, intolerable. Miss Ruth closed her prayer book, gathered her things, then rose to leave in the middle of the service. She leaned over to me, and in her best stage whisper said, "Martha, these people will get nowhere until they get a little theatricality."

She longed for the kind of theatricality that her friend the director King Vidor described when he suggested I go see revivalist Aimee Semple McPherson, in Los Angeles, at her Angelus Temple. I was very skeptical, but went to the performance. She entered dead center, dressed completely in white, holding dozens of crimson roses in her arms. When she reached the edge of the stage, she cried, "Stand up and kiss me," and dropped the roses before her. Even I found myself rising from my seat, captive.

Miss Ruth had the same quality that Nijinsky held, of being average offstage—not quite nondescript, but close—and then transforming themselves into a god or a goddess onstage. Miss Ruth could sit with me on a bus to the theatre cracking peanuts from an enormous sack, with shells all over her clothing, and then enter the theatre, complete her makeup and costume, and become the goddess figure. Of course, sometimes it was a little hard to tell which goddess she was. Part of the confusion was due to Pearl, her costumer, who was always a few sheets to the wind, and then more than a little befuddled.

Months before, while I was standing in the wings, Miss Ruth was about to enter to perform one of her most famous solos, "The Black and Gold Sari." Intuitively, without ever having seen East Indian dance, she created this solo, which she brought to India when the Indian dance was at its

84

lowest ebb. It was an extraordinary success and she was asked to help bring their art back to them. But that was yet to come. This particular night, when Miss Ruth was about to enter, a small group of girls was doing an innocuous dance onstage. Suddenly, Miss Ruth turned to me and said, "Martha, I cannot go on that stage. It's dead, so cold. Go find Pearl and have her give you a green and gold sari and get out there and do something. At the end, come toward me and salaam and I will make my entrance."

It went on like this for many weeks, until one evening in Cleveland I salaamed to Miss Ruth who had been gotten up by a more than usually inebriated Pearl. When I looked up Miss Ruth was in complete Japanese regalia—obi, wig, geta. We both gasped and exchanged looks of horror. As she hobbled off for the black and gold sari, she hissed at me, "Get back out and do something." It would have been easy for me to do her solo. I knew it inside out. But I did not, and after what seemed like an eternity, Miss Ruth appeared in the wings and I salaamed to her with a great relief. Perhaps this is why I have no patience for young dancers who have to be spoonfed every inch of the way.

In Pasadena, Miss Ruth was once in conversation with a matronly society woman, who had lots of bluing in her hair. Miss Ruth had been struggling to find the right headdress for her solo "The Peacock." As I watched Miss Ruth, I knew she was hearing nothing of what was said. Her eyes were focused on the hat the matron wore, with bird of paradise feathers and all sorts of plumage attached to it. Suddenly Miss Ruth said, "You don't mind, do you?" and reached up to take the feathers off the hat. "This will be perfect for my new dance."

Miss Ruth's mind was always on other things. Particularly that evening in Detroit, when in response to a standing ovation, she walked to the footlights, thanked the audience at great length and said, "For the rest of my performing days I will always keep in my heart, in memory of this reception of me, a special place for the wonderful people of Chicago."

But who could blame her? We performed so many one-night stands, rehearsing in the afternoon, returning to the theatre at night. After a while, every city begins to look the same.

Miss Ruth always wanted "a little more theatricality" in the costumes, which meant endless sewing of sequins and paillettes and appliqués, hour after hour. Finally, I don't know what possessed me. I was tired and exhausted, and said, "Miss Ruth, either I am to be a dancer or a seamstress. I cannot do both." She looked at me in shock. I was always so giving and fearful. She said, "Very well, Martha," and I never had to sew again.

86

We were out on speculation when Alexander Pantages came backstage to meet us to discuss the possibility of signing on with him. At the time, he was the biggest independent operator of vaudeville theatres in the country. Pantages was born in Greece, and as a child came to the United States after working in Cairo and on a steamer in the Mediterranean. When he came to the States, he went to San Francisco, and when the Klondike gold rush started in the late 1890s, he made his way to the Yukon, and there, his fortune.

Mr. Pantages was a little friendly, very friendly—you know, too friendly. He tried to kiss me, and I did not want it.

I said, "If I asked you, Mr. Pantages, if you wanted to kiss me and I didn't want you to, you wouldn't, would you?"

I was that young.

He said, "No, I guess I wouldn't. What do you want?"

"Mr. Pantages," I said, "I want to go to the top and I don't want to take anybody with me."

He said, "Come, little one. I'll sign your contract now." And he signed the contract.

I didn't know the top as I know it today. Then I just kept going on and danced and danced and danced. It was my passion. As I grew, I was recognized as a performer, a dancer. The top is a very bitter and wonderful thing. But it carries a lot of grief with it, too.

When the Denishawn company went to perform in London I was invited. It was Ted's idea to put Miss Ruth in my role as Xochitl. Although she had her own ideas about the dance and what she wanted to express through her own body, Ted insisted that they do Spanish dances and waltzes. He had gotten her to do dances that she never should have done. In a way, this was ruining her. It went against her spirit.

I received some wonderful reviews for my performances. Miss Ruth, however, did not. I used to worry that she would find my reviews, so I'd hide them. One time I was holding a few clippings in my hand when I heard Miss Ruth coming down the stairs. I hid because I was afraid that I would be sent away if she ever read them. I can still hear the sound of those footsteps getting fainter as I remained absolutely still.

I slept in a room next to Miss Ruth's that was divided by a partition that did not hit the ceiling. I would lie awake, because Miss Ruth was crying herself to sleep. The reviews were killing her. This was not what she wanted the dance to be. Ted was not the dancer or the innovator or the artist Miss Ruth was. I thought again of those footsteps I heard on the stairwell, how they descended like a whisper, getting weaker. Some great strength was growing fainter in Miss Ruth. It was a tragic, tragic moment. I wondered if I would ever suffer like that. I was that naive.

The nadir of the performances in London came when Ted got it into his head to dance Doris Humphrey's role in *Soaring*, a ballet to symbolize the birth of Venus from the sea foam. It began with an extrordinary sheer transparent piece of silk almost covering the stage, held at each end by young girls in blond Prince Valiant pageboys. I was one of them. We would lift the silk to catch the air and the slim suggestion of a body beneath it was Doris, rising and falling with the silk. The night Ted decided to play her role was the one night I did my part without once looking at the central figure. It was simply too horrible to encompass. And there was always the risk I might laugh.

When we returned to New York Ted took me down a certain street, turned a corner, and together we saw the headline on the lit marquee:

Xochitl *postcard with star billing,*
1920–21 season.

MARTHA GRAHAM IN XOCHITL. This was the first time I had ever seen my name in public. All I could think was, If only Mother and Father could see this.

My sister Geordie was with me in *Xochitl*, one of the six girls who danced with the fans. We traveled the country together on tour. At one stop, the conductor tried to put us off the train. He had called the police, sure that we were gypsies because of our clothes, jewelry, and our dark looks.

"No," I said to the officer who came aboard, "I will not leave the train and neither will my sister. We are not gypsies."

"We are the daughters of Dr. George Graham," Geordie said.

After a time we were believed and permitted to remain aboard the train, stay with the tour. The conductor apologized, but the drama of it all sustained us for months.

A now defunct dance magazine of the 1920s ran a cover story claiming that Geordie and I were not direct descendants of Miles Standish, but Romanian immigrants. Geordie and I arrived at their office like bats out of hell. Even though my strongest words were, and still are, "damnation" and "blue blazes," I gave them what for. Geordie exited with a particularly savory Irish insult, "I spit on you." It was always one of her favorites.

89

My youngest sister, Geordie, in East Indian costume, Denishawn.

When I left Denishawn to enter the *Greenwich Village Follies*, it was Geordie who took my place in *Xochitl* as it toured across the country. Once while touring America, Geordie ran a dangerously high temperature, but Ted and Miss Ruth put her onstage to dance the role of Xochitl; there was no understudy. Though Geordie was burning up, she did the dance, somehow, but collapsed afterward and nearly died. I never forgave Miss Ruth and Ted for that.

90

In New York at this time I would go to the Century Theatre on the Upper West Side to see Eleonora Duse who was appearing in a program that included Ibsen's *Ghosts* and *Così Sia* (Thy Will Be Done) by Gallarati Scotti. We never had much money and would go only to matinees and sit in the very top of the balcony. Duse was playing a mother whose baby was dying; she would suffer anything, if only his life could be saved. She said her prayers to the Madonna of Miracles. She wrapped her rosary around the arm of her son. She said, "Dear God, give me the life of this child. I will do anything. I will accept anything." Unfortunately, of course, the son later turned against her. Duse made one gesture while sitting in a large chair that made tears stream down my face. At the very end she realized the eternal futility of it all and simply turned her hand down. She had given everything for the life of this child, and nothing remained.

The *Greenwich Village Follies* was produced by John Murray Anderson. He saw me dance in New York during a Denishawn tour, which took us all around the country. I still have the clippings of our New York performance. The critics spoke of me as the only one in Ruth St. Denis's company to dance with passion and excitement. This, of course, did not sit too well with either Miss Ruth or Ted. To them I was still a nincompoop.

John Murray Anderson came to the studio one day to see every dance

I did. He had me do my complete repertoire. He was a very nice, very gentle, but very determined man. He taught beautifully and I learned a great deal from him. I learned to be theatrical in every sense of the word. And he meant theatrical. He was a great director with a great sense of tradition, and was not really appreciated enough.

Denishawn was preparing for their famous tour of the Orient and we were all excited by the prospect of the East. Geordie was chosen, but when I was called into the office, I was told I looked too Oriental and would not be a true representative of Denishawn. They wanted to bring an "all-American company"—blond hair and blue eyes. The peroxide bottles appeared for those not naturally what they called American. But I was damned if I would do that. They would leave for the East and I would be left alone. I was not frightened and thought of what my father said to me when I was younger: "Martha, you are a horse that runs best on a muddy track."

After I danced for John Murray Anderson he sat alone in the studio while I went to put a sweater on top of my dance clothes. When I returned we talked for a short time and then he offered me a role in the *Greenwich Village Follies* of 1923. I did not know what to say.

Denishawn was going to the Orient. My mother and Lizzie were in need of help in Santa Barbara—nothing could be done about the money that had been embezzled from Father's estate. I thought about it for a few minutes and then I said, "Yes, Mr. Anderson, I'd like to." It was a painful decision and I hope no one thinks I joined the *Follies* because I wanted to—I had no choice.

I had to be very careful with my finances at that time. They didn't pay you for rehearsal, only performances, and I had just enough money each day to take a bus to work at Columbus Circle and back to Fourteenth Street, or take a bus up and have lunch and walk back. I always chose lunch. Somehow I knew I would summon up the strength to walk home. Even pieces of paper were precious. To this day I cannot bear it if someone doesn't write on both sides of a piece of paper, or throws away a piece without using it. I wonder if that is where my image for the actors at the Neighborhood Playhouse came from. I would take a piece of paper and slowly rip it in half and tell them that was the tragedy of a piece of paper.

And then there was Mr. Anderson to contend with. As long as he liked you, you were all right. But if he didn't, gosh, you were a goner. During one rehearsal a group of showgirls had to prance across the stage in tiny costumes with ostrich plumes on their headbands. Mr. Anderson stopped the girls and said, "You look more like a funeral director's horses, except they were thoroughbreds." At another time, he just snarled at them, "And ladies, a little more virginity, if you please." But my all-time favorite was when he had been insulted by a society matron. He planned his revenge to the last detail. On alternate Mondays his opera box bordered this particular woman's. For the next evening, he sent his Irish maid, Rose, to the best makeup man and hairdresser, found her the most fabulous jewels, and sat her right in the middle of his box. To all the world, she looked like visiting royalty. She certainly did to the matron, who couldn't take her eyes off her. The next day, she telephoned Mr. Anderson and asked him to bring his guest to tea the following day. He answered, "You mean my maid. Oh, she will be so pleased to come. Of course we accept."

He chose me to play the girl in a production called "The Garden of Kama," a theatre piece based on Indian love lyrics. I was a fairy girl to the prince. I wore a sari and a choli. I might as well still have been in Denishawn.

This was very much a *Follies* piece. I ran up a flight of stairs—oh, so dramatic—threw open the door and turned my back to the audience. I lifted the dagger and stabbed myself and then dropped the dagger and fell, I thought beautifully, to the floor. The other solo was "Serenata Morisca," my first Denishawn solo, and the last was billed as "Moonlight Kisses." I danced in floating yellow chiffon, very Loie Fuller, while the great lovers of history, Romeo and Juliet, Tristan and Isolde, Antony and Cleopatra, and others paraded across a moonlit bridge.

We took "The Garden of Kama" on the road and one of the cities we stopped in was Boston, what we called "Boston town." And when you were in Boston, you behaved yourself. The blue laws were in effect at that time and so the girls in the production were not allowed to appear onstage in their outfits which consisted of rather small cholis. Every night a policeman would come to check the girls on the stage to see if they were wearing too scanty things. This big, very burly policeman said, "Put something on them so that they are respectable."

I was the leading dancer at this time and the showgirls hated me. In Chicago they nicknamed me the Princess, probably because I wouldn't talk with them; I was more than a little arrogant. I just didn't want to be there, but I had to be. And I never came down the runway at the end in that special dress. I was not a chorus girl or a hoofer. It came as no surprise when one of the showgirls who was told to cover up looked at me and said to the policeman, "Hey, what about her?" I thought I was in for it. I was wearing a good deal less than anyone there, and began to shiver because it was so cold backstage. "No, she's all right," he said. "She's art."

Shortly after, when we returned to New York, they wanted me in one of their scanty costumes, without a leotard to cover me underneath.

"No," I said, "I will wear my leotard."

"But you didn't with Denishawn," they protested.

"That was different," I said. "That was art."

Not all of the excitement in the *Follies* took place onstage. When my mother found out I was going into the *Follies* she appeared from California to be with me. She was protection. She would sleep in my bedroom. She saw to it that I remained a lady. I had had a very good upbringing, and I was a little bit outside the average girl of the *Follies*. They thought I was too good, you know. Too protected by my mother.

It seemed that Irene Delroy, the beautiful ingenue of the *Follies*, had

Newspaper cartoon of the Greenwich Village Follies.

not been so carefully brought up. She became the lover of Frankie Fay, a well-known gangster. He wouldn't allow anyone to touch her or be near her. He felt the same toward me. We were sacrosanct in his eyes. She had no other involvements but he was still insanely jealous. In Boston, Irene and I were walking down the street—she was supposed to be the most beautiful creature in the world, and she was—when two young Harvard students came up, took us in their arms, elevated us, and walked down the street with us. My mother was with us and almost died of the shame and fear she had because we were always under the watchful eyes of the gangster. He was told about this incident later.

"Did that man touch you?" he said to Irene.

"Did that man touch you? I will kill him," he said to me.

He never got angry with Irene or with me. He only got angry at any man who came near us.

I always went with them as their chaperon. Frankie insisted that I join them whenever they went out on the town and I was terrified to say no. How do you refuse a gangster? Frankie called me a lady. He wanted me to teach his girl to be the same.

Frankie always carried a gun. Many of his friends were shot at while having a drink with him. When we all went out together, Frankie would put his gun on the table. The waiters would say nothing, though they were face to face with a revolver. And the mood for the evening, to put it mildly, was tense.

It was the period of Prohibition and we would go into speakeasies. Whenever we appeared at a door and they saw Frankie Fay, we were escorted into the club and given a front table. It was a far cry from Santa Barbara. Dark and smoky, the clubs, or rooms that passed as clubs, had a sense of danger about them, and seduction.

The resentment of the showgirls continued to grow. For the finale, when the entire cast was onstage and the showgirls came down the runway to display themselves to the audience, rather like the *Ziegfeld Follies*, the girls wore elaborate, low-cut dresses. The sound of heavily beaded things would precede them into a room. The directors of the production were always trying to get me to wear one of those dresses and join the finale. One night the stage manager brought me drinks, which each time I poured into a plant near my dressing table when he left. I would have had to have a wooden leg to tolerate all that alcohol. I don't know what he thought, but it didn't weaken my resolve. Each time there was the same exchange—the stage manager would bring the dress for my finale entrance to my dressing room and I would say, "Take it back. I am not a showgirl." This kept them quiet for a time, but then they rolled in a rack of dresses for me to choose one. I was told that if I did not pick out one of these dresses to wear, one of my dances would be cut from the performance.

"Go ahead," I said. "But my solos stop the show every night."

And so they took out my solos for a few evenings until the stage manager reappeared in my dressing room. He glared at me and said, "Your solos are back."

"With the leotard?" I asked.

"With the leotard," he grudgingly agreed.

While on tour with the *Greenwich Village Follies* we went all over the country. Perhaps my greatest compliment came when I danced in the South—three solos a night in "Silk and Incense"—and a critic said I, among the other dancers, seemed like a wildflower in a garden of jazz.

Another critic said he had the feeling that had there been no music or no stage or no lights, Martha Graham like an East Indian priestess still would have been dancing for her gods. I was what the Indians called a devidassi, a temple dancer.

I traveled with the *Greenwich Village Follies* to London, where we were a huge success. We were touring on a vaudeville circuit, and our act went on just before Miss May's white horses. Once, I was in the wings, preparing to make an entrance, when suddenly I

96

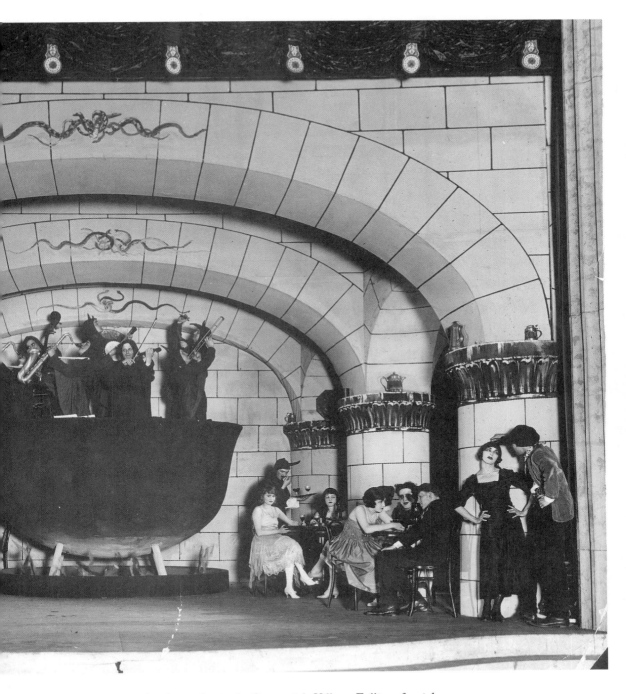

Dancing an Apache number in the Greenwich Village Follies, *far right.*

felt a big sloppy kiss on my bare shoulder. I turned around and it was one of Miss May's beautiful show horses.

There was a parrot named Ethel who was caged until it was time for her performance. We all shared the same dark area backstage. But poor Ethel tore all her feathers out—the ones remaining of the many she had simply lost because of her age. Whenever Ethel heard her music, which meant it was time for her to go on, she would try and tear her cage apart. She was that anxious to perform. When I was about to go on, I turned to one of the stagehands near me and said, "I understand Ethel now."

One of our stops when I toured the states with the *Follies* was Chicago. I remember going into the Art Institute one afternoon. I entered a room where the first modern paintings I had ever seen were on display—Chagalls and Matisses—and something within me responded to those paintings. I saw across the room a beautiful painting, what was then called abstract art, a startling new idea. I nearly fainted because at that moment I knew I was not mad, that others saw the world, saw art, the way I did. It was by Wassily Kandinsky, and had a streak of red going from one end to the other. I said, "I will do that someday. I will make a dance like that."

And I did. I didn't know it at the time, but it had such a great influence on me; that shaft of intimacy. The dance was *Diversion of Angels*. It happened one rainy summer at Connecticut College in 1948, and I thought no angel would ever appear in that weather. *Diversion* is about the love of life and the love of love; the meeting and the parting of a man and a woman. There is a woman in white who symbolizes mature love. She is only able to move in balance with her partner, her lover. There is a girl in yellow who is adolescent love; and a woman in red, who flashes across the stage as erotic love. All are aspects of the same woman, and the girl in red is the Kandinsky flame I had seen so long ago at the Chicago Art Institute.

It's very hard to dance the woman in red. She has to have a curious vulnerability, almost like a breathlessness and a deep eroticism. Many people can't get it, they go rocking from one side to the other side and on and on. But it is a constant rediscovering of the focused instant.

There is a quote from Genesis that I recite to the dancers for *Diversion*: "The sons of God saw the daughters of men that they were fair; and they took them wives of all that they chose."

"You're sons of God," I'd say, "angels all of you."

Dance followed modern painters and architects in discarding decorative essentials and fancy trimmings. Dance was not to be "pretty" but much more real.

I had my first lighting lesson in the *Follies* when we prepared for a gala fund-raiser, much like a vaudeville show. Each performer went to the lighting designer with the most god-awful complicated instructions—follow me in a soft blue, then fade to a dead white, and so on. One dancer came up to ask for her lighting and said simply, "Listen. When I get out there, take a number sixteen lavender spotlight and just follow me." He did, and she had the best lighting in the show.

Jean Rosenthal, who went on to become one of the greatest innovators in lighting in the theatre, came to me as a young girl and wanted to be a dancer. Soon, it was clear to both of us that this was not her path. I suggested lighting and for years she would work with me and experiment. Rosenthal blue, that vibrant backdrop that soon became almost standard background in theatre production, had its start when Jean created it for me, when I first did *Appalachian Spring* in 1944. I needed a clear blue American sky—uncluttered, simple, no kitsch or effects, and that is what Jean brought me.

When Jean was dying of cancer she made the most extraordinary gesture. In April 1969 I had completed, as much as any work of art is

Appalachian Spring *with Erick Hawkins, Merce Cunningham, and May O'Donnell,* *October 30, 1944.*

completed, my ballet *Archaic Hours*, and Jean got permission to come out of the hospital in an ambulance. She sat on a stretcher with me in the aisle of the City Center Theatre and supervised the last work she would ever light.

Jean loved to tease about lighting me. She would say, I never have to worry about lighting Martha because she always goes to the light. Jean's lighting was perfect, but I still longed for the days before brilliant lighting and false eyelashes, when Sarah Bernhardt would bead her lashes (something I did until very late in my career). The beading was colored wax that was melted from a candle over a flame and brushed onto the eyelashes. When the soft lights hit those lashes, it was almost as if you were wearing crystals.

Bernhardt made a tremendous mark on my life. When I saw her perform, she had just survived the amputation of her leg and, onstage, was dressed in her costume for *L'Aiglon*. She recited her great speech on the battlefield of Wagram, and her voice was beautiful, beyond beautiful, if possible. Bernhardt's voice was golden.

Greenwich Village Follies dancers were always asked to perform at private homes and for the most part I resisted. "I had me pride," too much at times, but the invitation to perform at one of those vast marble mansions in Newport, Rhode Island, had its appeal. Though I had no money, I was determined to arrive in style. I borrowed money from my dresser to rent a chauffeur-driven car, and she agreed to travel with me as my maid. When we arrived the butler said that as an artist I was to enter through the servants' entrance. I absolutely refused and told him I would arrive as I saw fit, with the other guests, or return that instant to New York City. The other performer did what she was told, but I was permitted to enter through the front doors. At the end of the evening, she returned to New York, but I was asked by my hosts to stay overnight and remain for supper the next evening.

Years later I returned to Newport and was showered with great luxury and kindness by my friend Doris Duke at her house on the cliffs. If Miss Ruth would have seen Doris, she would have made her a Denishawn dancer, with her exotic looks and sinuous way of moving.

While I was in the *Follies* I always had dinner alone because there was no one with whom I could feel comfortable. I would go to a Chinese restaurant and order my meals. Once, a young waiter said, "You're Chinese."

I said, "No."

He said, "Your papa Chinese?"

I said, "No."

He said, "Your mama Chinese?"

I said, "No."

He said, "Where do you come from?"

"California."

"Ah" he said. "You come from San Francisco. You are Chinese." So he got his meal and sat down with me as a friend and we ate our meal together. At least he didn't suggest I dance an Oriental flower arranger. I was accepted as Chinese. I do not fully understand or encompass when this happens. It has only to do with my form, not with what I really am.

I had a Chinese girl in one of my classes who had some difficulty in attending because her mother did not want her to study with me. I could not figure out why, as she was a very talented dancer. Finally, her mother saw a performance of the company. She did not like it.

Her only comment to her daughter after meeting me was "Martha Graham has been very well brought up by her mother and father."

"This woman changes. She is Tao," her mother later said. And that was that.

Her mother feared this element of change. Change is the only constant. You see, when you put your foot in a stream of water, you can't put it in the same stream twice, because that's gone. You're in a new place in the stream. The Chinese have a sense of change: change not deliberately to change but because time invokes changes and enables you to go on. I believe in change because it's so eternal. It doesn't stay in one place. It's constant growth. Constant rebirth.

As I grow older, people, even reserved Orientals, are very fond of kissing me. I don't like being kissed very much. Even in the old days I waited for the real thing, yet people will come and kiss me on the cheek. It is an act of possession. They take a bit, just like the apple dance in *El Penitente*. "Do you want a bite? It is here for the taking."

· · ·

At one time I was preparing to go onstage with the *Follies* and was dressing with a wonderful Spanish family, Eduardo and Volga Cansino. While I was putting on my makeup their little girl, Margarita, who was perhaps five or six years old, would crawl under my chair. She was raised in the theatre and grew up to become Rita Hayworth.

The *Follies* served a purpose, but I knew there was something else for me to do. I remember once up in the Bronx, I had spent the night with a boyfriend and while I was washing my hands in the sink it suddenly dawned on me that I was not about my Father's business. That, of course, is biblical, but I did believe that if you followed what you believed to be beautiful, you would achieve what you were supposed to achieve.

I did not enjoy the *Follies*, yet in some ways I did. I danced four solos a night. I had billing and the salary was a high one. I was considered an exotic personality onstage (at least in that it resembled Denishawn) and to my delight, each night one of my solos would stop the show.

The *Follies* was a completely professional thing. We did at least five shows a night, even on Sundays. It was a discipline Denishawn had prepared me for and I continued to learn the mood and the feeling of the audience. But more often than not, I cried myself to sleep. It was not where I chose to be. It was my responsibility to be there to support my family. I left in 1925, when I wanted to create my own dances, on my own body.

When I came out of the *Follies* I had no place to go in New York. At the Metropolitan Museum it was forbidden to go and sit among the Egyptian things. I walked to the Central Park zoo and sat on a bench across from a lion in its cage. It would go from one side of the cage to the other. It repeatedly made the footprints four times over and back. It was a wonderful way that it turned to go. I would watch this lion for hours as he'd take those great padding steps four times back and across the cage. Finally, I learned to walk that way. I learned from the lion the inevitability of return, the shifting of one's body. The shift of the weight is one key aspect of that technique, that manner of movement. George Balanchine once said that mine was classical technique. I cherished those words. It meant it was not a momentary eccentricity, but a scientific thing that could be transmitted from one dance generation to the next.

At this time, I did not have what is known as a technique. I was fresh from the *Follies*. But in the technique that would later evolve the weight is shifted in the strange animal way that is not ballet but contemporary dance—the shift of the weight that is so key to the movement.

104

With a lion cub in a California park.

In a way, we have lost the quality of an animal through our sense of safety, but like animals the body must always be able to move from one position to another.

Years later, I would think of that lion and the strange and powerful way in which he moved. My company and I were at Stonehenge. We took a bus early one morning from London to Salisbury Plain in order to get to Stonehenge before dawn. I had dreamed of it. I had been told of it, and suddenly I was very shocked to see this group of rocks. There was nothing there except the complete isolation and mystery of the structure. No one knows why it was brought there, or how it was used. I had a feeling of the dark night of the soul when one wanders through the intricacies of doubt and fear and searching and there's nothing to be found anyplace except among these immense silent structures. When I first was at Stonehenge, you could walk around. You could sit on the altar where the sun came in every day and struck a man's heart as the sacrificial animal. But today it's all fenced off.

I stood with Takako Asakawa, a dancer in my company, in the doorway through which the light penetrated to the slab which is believed to be the sacrificial rock. The light struck at the height of the heart. To make certain of this I lay down on the rock, and though it was not dawn, the light seemed to strike directly into my heart. I felt free to wander around. I was puzzled, just like everyone else there, and I was overwhelmed by the mystery.

Takako and I walked through this huddle of strange stone shapes until we reached the cathedral. There was a choral performance in progress. The choir sat on either side of the entranceway, while the choirmaster walked between them with a stick and directed them. Takako said in her strange Japanese way, "They know we come?"

I said, "No. Listen." Something very wonderful, some music was being called forth.

The choir was singing a very ancient thing, but slowly it became familiar. It was taken up by the Quakers and called "The Gift to Be Simple." It was the hymn I had asked Aaron Copland to place at a point in the score of *Appalachian Spring*.

I remember the last time we went to Stonehenge, when we could not walk through the history of stone. Everyone said, "How will we know where the sun will strike?"

I said, "Look at the cows."

One by one they rose and stood looking into the darkness seconds before the dawn and then turned to look into the light that pierced the entrance to Stonehenge.

Strange formations have always obsessed me because they are the emanation of the power of the world which is creating us and which is

creating new worlds at this moment. And the rocks—the millions of years
. . . How could anyone know that an island was being formed, which
would not emerge for two or three million years? But that surge was there.

I accepted a teaching job at the Eastman School of Dance in Rochester,
New York, at the invitation of Rouben Mamoulian, in the fall of 1925.
The Russian-born director, formerly associated with Stanislavsky's Mos-
cow Art Theatre, had arrived in the United States only a year or so earlier.
He embarked on a series of operas and motion-picture stage shows for
film king George Eastman in Rochester.

"Dance," he once said, "is the foundation of the theatre."

I went to Rochester with Louis Horst, who left Denishawn about the
same time that I left the *Follies*. He had gone to Vienna to study music,
but returned shortly afterward to the States. We came down a path to
meet Rouben Mamoulian, who said we arrived like Salome and John the
Baptist.

Esther Gustafson, the teacher who preceded me in Rochester, was
what was then called a nature dancer, emphasizing all that was natural in
movement, in clothes, very restrained and proper, no makeup to speak of.
She gave the impression that she thought eyeliner was an instrument of
the devil.

I entered my first class in a clinging red silk kimono, with a long slit
up each leg, a full makeup, my hair pulled back severely but dramatically.
The students, who were used to their Swedish teacher's more down-to-
earth approach, were in a state of shock after the class. "Well," I told
Rouben, "they needed it."

I learned a great deal at Rochester, but not enough to keep my interest
or speak to what I was passionate about—finding my own way as a dancer.
They were generous. I had my own studio and all the students I could
wish. And yet I was troubled and restless. What the people in Rochester

did not understand was that dance was going to develop into an art, and not remain an entertainment in the spirit of Radio City Music Hall. They wanted revues suitable for the Eastman Theatre.

The first dances I made at Rochester were not terribly original and were very derivative of Denishawn, but that was all I knew. When I was asked to make a dance for the Eastman laboratory to film with the new, experimental, color motion-picture film, I agreed, never realizing that the dreadful thing would resurface years later. It was called "Flute of Krishna." Perhaps I am being too hard on it. It was, after all, meant to be frankly decorative. The trio of dancers I worked with, Evelyn Sabin, Thelma

107

My first company of dancers, who studied with me at the Eastman School, Rochester.

Biracree, and Betty Macdonald, would dance with me in my first New York concert, one year later.

When the time came to renew my contract for a second year, it was a very difficult decision. As I walked into the huge room, I thought I was ruining myself just for the money. I approached the desk, picked up the fountain pen, and started to sign my name. I got as far as the M, then put the pen back down on the desk.

"Excuse me, Mr. Hanson, I cannot do this." I turned, walked out, packed my things, and returned to Manhattan. I would do anything for dance, but not this.

I wanted something more from dance. It used to be that when dance was staged, a flurry of the hand meant nothing more than the representation of falling rain. The arm, moved in a certain way, suggested a wildflower or the growth of corn. Why, though, should an arm try to be corn, or a hand, rain? The hand is too wonderful a thing to be an imitation of something else.

At this time, I could not afford to buy books but would always go to the Gotham Book Mart on West Forty-seventh Street, which was owned by Frances Steloff. She had been a little Jewish immigrant girl from Russia, who was so poor in Saratoga Springs she sold flowers to make money. She just loved books and had this great respect for knowledge. She used to give me books to take home because I couldn't afford them. She had a blond cat that wandered everyplace, all over the tables and the piles of books.

Frances was very generous with the writers and other artists of the time. No one had much money then. I remember once when Edmund Wilson came into the shop. He said, "Frances, I need to cash a check."

Frances said, "Now, Edmund, don't bother me, I'm busy. Just go to the cash register and take what you need and leave a little piece of paper saying how much it is."

Early dance study by Soichi Sunami.

I was so impressed by this I almost fainted dead away. He went to the cash register, took what he needed, and left.

During one particularly hectic Christmas I assisted Frances in the store. A sailor came in and I helped him find a book he was searching for. When Frances put me on the cash register I did something wrong to ruin the roll of tape that wound around it. The customers began to line up at the front desk until Frances came to my rescue. I would also help wrap books, because at this time they were not put in bags but were wrapped with paper and twine.

Frances believed in me and without ever having seen me dance signed a loan for one thousand dollars for my first concert. I was a nobody, but I was given one chance to prove myself. I wanted to gamble on being judged on Broadway, and not perform in my studio just for friends. I went to Mr. Green, of the *Greenwich Village Follies*, and asked him if I could have his theatre for one night, just to show what I could do. He said, "Yes, you can. If you fail, you will go back into the *Follies* for one year." We could use his theatre on a Sunday, but the show had to be billed as a sacred concert because of the blue laws forbidding dance performances.

That first concert was held at the 48th Street Theatre on April 18, 1926. I danced solos to the music of Schumann, Debussy, Ravel, and others. Louis Horst was my accompanist. With my trio of girls from Rochester, we danced "Chorale" to the music of Cesar Franck and "Clair de lune" to the music of Claude Debussy. I did many dances, and everything I did was influenced by Denishawn. There was an audience. They came because I was such a curiosity—a woman who could do her own work. Although there was a snowstorm that night, at the second intermission Mr. Green came backstage and said, "You made it." I didn't have to return. My path was clear.

· · ·

From my first concert in New York City, April 18, 1926.

A Study in Lacquer, *first concert, April 18, 1926.*

One woman, a friend of Miss Ruth's who had seen me dance at Denishawn, came backstage after my first solo performance. She was dressed as a woman of the late nineteenth century. She wore a many-layered, cluttered

Scène Javanaise, *Rochester, New York, May 27, 1926.*

dress, a fur hat with feathers on it, great beads and all. She said, "Martha, this is simply dreadful. How long do you expect to keep this up?"

I said, "As long as I've got an audience."

That's been my criterion. Sometimes the audiences have been very small, but they have sustained me. The response of Miss Ruth's friend was typical. To many people, I was a heretic. A heretic is a woman who is put upon in all she does, a woman who is frightened. Everyplace she goes she goes against the heavy beat and footsteps of those she opposes. Maybe she is a heretic in a religious way, maybe in a social way. I felt at the time that I was a heretic. I was outside of the realm of women. I did not dance the way that people danced. I had what I called a contraction and a release. I used the floor. I used the flexed foot. I showed effort. My foot was bare. In many ways I showed onstage what most people came to the theatre to avoid.

Three years later I created a dance called *Heretic*. I decided that morning that the costumes were wrong. I went down to the Lower East Side, to Delancey Street to my favorite fabric shop, and bought wool jersey for eighteen cents a yard. I went back to the studio, we made our costumes, and by evening we were ready. Onstage I danced the woman in white, while the others in my company were dressed in black. They became a wall of defiance that I could not break. The music, an old Breton song, would stop, and the women in black formed another group. I was the heretic desperately trying to force myself free of the darkness of my oppressors.

I had made up my mind that I was going to rely on the audience, on people who bought tickets, not just on those whom I had invited and who wanted me to succeed. Some people did not. They thought I was extremely ugly and that I did some dreadful things.

I remember years later my mother said to me, "Martha, I don't see why you have to present such dreadful women on the stage. You're really rather sweet when you're at home."

I'd rather an audience like me than dislike me, but I'd rather they disliked me than be apathetic, because that is the kiss of death. I know because I have had both . . .

Désir, *Klaw Theatre, New York, November 28, 1926.*

Three Poems of the East, *November 28, 1926.*

Heretic, *April 14, 1929.*

Lamentation, my dance of 1930, is a solo piece in which I wear a long tube of material to indicate the tragedy that obsesses the body, the ability to stretch inside your own skin, to witness and test the perimeters and boundaries of grief, which is honorable and universal. I was backstage, changing out of my costume and removing my makeup, when there was a knock at the door. A woman entered my dressing room. She had obviously been crying a great deal and she said to me, "You will never know what you have done for me tonight. Thank you."

She left before I could get her name. Later I learned that she had recently seen her nine-year-old son killed by a truck before her eyes. She was unable to cry. No matter what was done for her she was not able to cry until she watched *Lamentation*. What I learned that night is that there is always one person in the audience to whom you speak. One. All I ask is that you feel for or against.

Another time I was doing *Lamentation* in the South and got a completely different response. I danced on a small stage at an exclusive women's club. One disgruntled old lady got out of her chair and made her way toward me down the empty aisle of the auditorium. She put her hands on the stage and looked at me. Then she turned around and walked out. That was that . . . but I finished the dance.

There is a wonderful Icelandic term: "doom eager." You are doom eager for destiny no matter what it costs you. The ordeal of isolation, the ordeal of loneliness, the ordeal of doubt, the ordeal of vulnerability which it takes to compose in any medium, is hard to face. You know when this thing is coming on you. You know when you walk the streets by the hour. When the restlessness comes, when you are sick with an idea, with something that will not come out.

Robert Edmond Jones, a visionary designer and director, who taught at the Neighborhood Playhouse, would begin his first lecture to his students by slowly, silently looking at each and every one, back and forth, almost with the pacing, inevitable rhythm of a lion in a cage. And then suddenly he would cry, "I am studying you very carefully because I know here in this room there are a few, only a few, who are doom eager . . . doom eager to be an artist." And the artist is doom eager, but never chooses his fate. He is chosen, and anointed, and caught.

Lamentation, *January 8, 1930.*

I felt I had to grow and work within myself. I wanted, in all my arrogance, to do something in dance uniquely American. I found one dance pupil and that began it. She was Bernard Berenson's niece from Italy. And then I had a few more girls to teach. They found out that they could go to this place, not costing too much, and could learn something and have fun doing it. I did not teach the technique classes that I learned at the Denishawn school for the simple reason that I could not afford the five-hundred-dollar fee they demanded from anyone who taught their method. I taught on my own, and soon afterward Louis Horst and I began to teach classes at the Neighborhood Playhouse.

I taught a very strict technical class in movement for actors. I tempered it down a bit from what I would teach a dancer, but I always treated them as students, and for the most part they were not famous yet—whether it was Bette Davis or Gregory Peck or, later, Liza Minnelli and Woody Allen. Joanne Woodward was one of my students. She told me of her first class there. She and Tony Randall and others were not too happy about it. They nicknamed it "gym." I apparently entered the room and they didn't quiet down. Joanne said I simply stood there very strong and proud and still, until, without looking at them, I sensed they were settling down and staring at me. Joanne remembered that I said, with perfect timing, "There are tears rolling down inside my cheeks." With that, I had them. They all wanted that kind of power and drama. Whether they got it or not was another matter.

Joanne was kind enough to say that class helped her when she played the multiple-personality character in *Three Faces of Eve* that won her an Oscar. She was at first perplexed with what to do; then she remembered class and played one character in contraction (breathe out, expelled), one in normal stance, and one in release (breathe in, into the body).

When Gregory Peck first came to the Playhouse he was a gangling young man in his twenties, clear and etched, very pure and very handsome. He was very hungry, too. Not only for the classes, but in need of a good meal. I asked him if he had enough to live and he mentioned a very small sum, barely enough to subsist on. When I asked what he really needed, he mentioned an equally small amount. It was just like Greg. I marched straight into the director's office, asked for something for him, and she agreed.

At the John Murray Anderson school Bette Davis was outspoken and said exactly what was on her mind. She moved and spoke with courage. The minute I saw her feet I knew she was destined for stardom. She was cooperative in a certain way, a very good pupil. She tried hard to do everything as it should be done. She wasn't in any way difficult.

Actors wanted to know their bodies. One man in class was asked to recite Hamlet's "To Be or Not to Be" soliloquy. It came out so prissy, so unmasculine: To-Be-or-Not-to-Be-That-Is-the-Question. I put him with one leg on the barre and his head to his knee and asked him to say the line again.

Then I said to him, "Get up and do that line as you did it at the barre." And it came out the way it should.

It was at that time I coached Ingrid Bergman privately. I remember that she had these exceedingly long silences. But I do love what she said was her secret of a happy life—good health and a bad memory.

One day in the early 1970s I walked into the studio and my assistant said, "Woody Allen is here taking class."

"Impossible," I said.

But there he was. He was doing some turns, he was doing splits, then running across the floor. Woody recently contributed a quote for our student brochure when asked to describe what it was like to have class in the Martha Graham technique:

"For me it was very serious, for the others watching me it was hilarious."

Woody surprised me when he asked if he could use our studio for the audition scene in *Annie Hall*. I, of course, agreed and refused any payment.

But when I went to see the film and the scene came, all I could do was lower my head in shame, for the baseboards had not been cleaned.

When I first came to the Neighborhood Playhouse downtown I saw a performance of a Burmese woman on a newsreel. The film was made by a man named Sandanee. The woman was wearing the same costume that I wore at Denishawn—a yellow Burmese skirt and a little white jacket. Everything we did at Denishawn was completely accurate. She was preparing herself to fight a cobra. It was the same ritual in which her sister, a priestess as well, had died. There had been no male child born in this town in Burma for two years. So it was her role as a priestess to dance with the cobra. Once it came out of its cave the woman began to dance with him. He became so enthralled with her dance. She would hold up her sari and the snake would strike the sari. He spent his venom, so that her skirt was absolutely pale with the stuff. He became so inert and so physically done with the spending of the venom that she lifted his head and she kissed him three times on the mouth and the ceremony was completed.

Movement never lies. The body is a very strange business. The chakras awake the centers of energy in the body, as in kundalini yoga. The awakening starts in the feet and goes up. Through the torso, the neck, up, up, through the head, all the while releasing energy. I've used this too, in a very naughty way, to defeat a man who bored me. I looked at his feet, then I continued to look slowly all the way up his body to his face and then turned away. He did not interest me.

I was doing a dance from Bloch's *Contrition and Rejoicing*—a forerunner of *Lamentation*, I was doing it against the wall of my studio in Carnegie Hall, room 107, and I had a shawl over my head. Evidently, I identified so

Ekstasis, *May 4, 1933*.

strongly with it that I fainted. When I woke it was quite dim, late afternoon, and I knew that I had been out for quite a few hours.

When I was making a dance called *Ekstasis* in 1933, I discovered, for myself, the relationship between the hip and the shoulder. I wore a tube of jersey which made me more aware of the stretching of the body and the articulation of anatomy. Each part is in its own way dramatic.

It was at this period that I was doing what critics called my long woolen dances of revolt, and looking back at them, they were pretty revolting. But I was really casting off Denishawn and its veils and exoticism with a vengeance, as most children do when they leave home. I was expressing something within me I didn't fully understand.

As with a child, as with a little animal that has to be trained, there has to be discipline and it has to be consistent. You rebel against it, but you enjoy the boundaries. And there's a will to do things of which we're completely unconscious—it is the force of life using us as a channel, and we have to submit to that. We are an instrument. I have to tell you that I didn't feel I was submitting. I didn't think I was denying myself. I enjoyed it. I enjoyed all the time I was working on the floor or in front of the mirror. I never felt tied down, humiliated, deprived. I felt I was very fortunate; I still feel that.

When I had a choreographic block and would begin to panic, I would leave my studio and walk through the old John Wanamaker department store, where Suzy the monkey lived in a cage upstairs. At this time, Wanamaker's was considered very ultra-ultra in its ability to house an ape in a cage, for people to come and see. I used to enjoy going to the store to see Suzy, who was very interesting and very independent. She had platforms and rocks to perform on, even bars where she could swing above the height of the crowd that came to see her. She would emerge and look at the people gathered, but if the audience was sparse or unresponsive, Suzy would retire to the cave at the rear of the cage and, I imagine, go to sleep. She had counted the house.

It reminded me of the times my parents would take me to the Wanamaker's in Pittsburgh, when I was a child. There we'd make a special visit to a grand room of polished wood and shining metals, where I was to absolutely behave. And I would, for the most part, because I wanted to return. We'd each sit on a tall stool at a soda fountain counter and eat a charlotte russe—a great whipped-cream kind of confection with a sponge cake underneath. It took a tall spoon to get to the very bottom of this dessert. My feet, I remember, were not even close to touching the ground.

·   ·   ·

I never read a review at the beginning. Sometimes I would not read the review for months, because I had my own ideas of what I had to say and the critics went by the wayside. The critic thinks that he is giving me to the public. He is not.

He's giving his idea of me to the public. It can be harmful. It can be helpful. But it has never influenced me.

I remember once giving a performance at the Martin Beck Theatre, and there was a terrific snowstorm that kept all of us backstage, not knowing if there would be a performance. We paced nervously, peeking through the house curtain when we could. But then the seats began to fill up, and we soon sold out. Someone said to Martin Beck, "Have you ever seen Martha Graham dance?"

"No," he said. "Why should I? She filled the house."

That was pretty much the attitude of the time. What mattered was that you were good box office. And we were.

I will never forget what the English ballet dancer and choreographer Frederick Ashton said about me. Ashton was generally considered the most important creative dancer in Britain, and later he became director of the Royal Ballet.

Ashton and his friends were in the audience of the Little Theatre in New York in 1927 when I danced *Revolt*, with music by Arthur Honegger. Frederick's friends did not like what they were seeing, schooled as they were in the traditions of Marie Rambert, who had danced with Nijinsky.

They wanted to leave the performance before the intermission, but Frederick just turned to his friends and said, "She is all right. She is theatrical." I was, at this point, fresh from the *Follies* and years of Denishawn. Some of the movements that I had evolved, or that they tell me I had evolved, were not creations, they were slight remembrances. They were awkward, they were probably unbeautiful in the terms that the world had seen in dancing at that time. Even Fanny Brice did a spoof of *Revolt* in the *Ziegfeld Follies*, called "Rewolt."

She danced to a piece of music called "Modernistic Moe," and she was

a great satirist. Nothing vulgar about her at all. She had evidently seen some of my performances. As a perfect mimic she copied my makeup, hair, costumes, facial expression, and all my severity. The girls in the chorus were exact copies of my girls. I think she was doing a combination of *Heretic* and *Celebration*. She came out singing, "Jumping, jumping, jumping" with all the girls behind her jumping . . . and at the very end she rushed to the footlights, put her hands out, just as I did in a ballet called *Act of Piety*, and with that wonderful Yiddish accent of hers cried out "Rewolt." I went back to four performances, but I never had the courage to go backstage. Danny Kaye did a takeoff of me in some revue, with his Graham Crackers. But my own favorite was something Cyril Ritchard did in an English revue. He had himself completely done up in my hair and makeup and did a hysterical send-up of *Frontier*. I've never really warmed to the idea of female impersonators, but then I sort of have to agree with Mae West, who said, "What's wrong with it? Women have been doing it for years."

In 1930, Leopold Stokowski invited me to dance the role of Élue, the Chosen One, in *The Rite of Spring* (*Le Sacre du Printemps*), though I had only danced on my own for a couple of years. I was performing at the Roerich Museum, on the Upper West Side of Manhattan, and Stokowski and his then wife, Evangeline, came to see me. He approached me about *Le Sacre* but was reticent about my doing the choreography. He did not think I had enough experience and I agreed.

When Nijinsky's original production of *Le Sacre* premiered in Paris in 1913, the strange choreography coupled with Stravinsky's music created havoc in the theatre. One proper, older woman was sitting next to a man who applauded enthusiastically at the newness of the movement and the sound. She turned and hit him on the head with her umbrella. She, like most of Paris, was completely shocked by the outrage of the music. I met

Two Primitive Canticles, *February 2, 1931.*

Revolt, *October 16, 1927.*

Stravinsky once, but I was a nobody, and he barely acknowledged my presence. He was in a great anger at the moment, not at me, but at the world.

Soon afterward, Stokowski decided that Léonide Massine would choreograph *Le Sacre*, since he was responsible for the success of the 1920 Paris revival. Massine was a thin man with very dark hair and striking features. His wife was the ballerina Eugenia Delarova. I first met him during the Depression when he came to my apartment in Manhattan. It was small and relatively inexpensive, and I got it because, frankly, nobody else wanted it. It was bare, no real furniture to speak of but an army cot, a chest of drawers with a Madonna, a small linoleum kitchen table, and a Victrola. Together we listened to *Le Sacre* while we looked out at the gray expanse of the city.

We agreed to work together. He was reconstructing the ballet and he frankly did not like me. We had many of our rehearsals at the Dalton School. Every time I did my solo he would turn his back on me, which is a big help, you know. During rehearsals, someone commented that Massine and I looked alike—we were both thin and dark and could have been mistaken for siblings. He was generous with me at the start, but after a time he asked me to resign. He thought I was going to fail. His mistress at the time, he felt, would be just right. Nothing could move me to resign. The more he ignored me, the more he came up to me when I was seated on the floor and whispered, "You should withdraw. You will have a terrible disaster if you are not a classical ballet dancer," the more I wanted to stay. Stokowski was firm and said I would dance Élue.

The first performance was in Philadelphia, on April 11, 1930, and we returned to New York by train to appear at the Metropolitan Opera House on April 22 and 23. Massine asked me what I thought was wrong. I said, "First, get rid of those dreadful buttercups in the background." He said that he could not. What else? "Well," I said, "I always thought the Chosen One should enter in the first section [something I finally did in my own

129

Dancing the Chosen One in The Rite of Spring, *presented at the Metropolitan Opera House in New York and in Philadelphia, April 1930.*

version in 1984], and it is impossible to be convincing about anything in those dreadful boots and wig I have to wear." Stokowski agreed, much to Massine's dismay, and I used my practice dress for the performance and my own hair, which came down to my waist.

It was a very trying time for me because I was not accepted. I was an outsider. I did exactly what Massine told me to do. I interpreted nothing of my own except some qualities of emotion.

I did not always agree with Stokowski, but he was for me a master. I was in awe of him. But I could not do certain things he wanted. After a disagreement he came into the studio when I was with a group of people and apologized. I said, "The Master can do no wrong," and he backed away.

We were together once in one of the pueblos in the Southwest. He was wearing walking shorts. The Indians in this particular pueblo had never seen anyone in shorts before. They were fascinated, and since he seemed more than a little pompous to them, they decided to have some playful fun with him. We were watching an Indian dance ceremony when Stokowski turned to me and said, "Let me explain this to you. This is called the Skunk Dance." When the Indians heard this they collapsed in laughter. I spoke to the Indians and said, "You have been very naughty telling the Maestro such a story. You must tell him the truth, that this is the Corn Dance."

For the most part my visits with Stokowski were amiable—almost too amiable until I put a stop to it. One evening he and Evangeline invited me to supper. She slipped out shortly afterward. The lights dimmed. I knew instantly it was a setup. When his hand reached to my knee, I looked at him from the feet up, very, very slowly, and said, "But, Maestro, I never dreamed there would ever be anything like this between us." And that ended it.

Alfred Stieglitz had come to see *The Rite of Spring* at the Metropolitan Opera House. Soon after, I went to his gallery at 291 Fifth Avenue. Though I knew the paintings and photographs that hung there, I was not particularly interested in the social lives of these artists. I was working eight hours a day. I had to work in order to support my mother and Lizzie in California. I had to get up at six in the morning to work with the pianist I had. It was the only time of day we both could spare. Afterward, I would rest a little, then begin to teach my classes.

Alfred had a cot that he sat on in the gallery. He was not well and he would rest a great deal. He started to talk about the production of *The Rite of Spring* and my role as the Chosen One. He felt that it was beneath my strength as a dancer.

With Lotte Lehmann and Leopold Stokowski outside the Santa Barbara Opera House.

"I don't approve of what you are doing," he said.

"Neither do I," I replied.

Some years later when I visited him again in his gallery he offered me a beautiful flower painting by his wife, Georgia O'Keeffe.

"Would you like to borrow it?" he asked.

I said, "No. I just live in a walk-up flat and I'm afraid that anything so valuable would be taken."

But I could visit Alfred as often as I liked, and many times we would sit together and he would read passages from Georgia's glorious letters. I remember one vividly about her waking just before dawn to bake bread in her adobe oven.

I first met Georgia O'Keeffe in Santa Fe, though we were never really close friends. In New York, I asked her once to let me use one of her sensual flower paintings as a backdrop in a new work I was trying to do. She refused because she felt that it had nothing to do with the dance. And from that point on, I have tried to avoid a painting or a backdrop of any kind.

133

My second studio, after Carnegie Hall, was at 66 Fifth Avenue in Greenwich Village. I rented my fourth-floor space from a Mr. Kaplan. He was a very kind man, which was fortunate for me because many times I was late in my rent. "Let her alone, she'll pay," he always said when one of his partners wanted me out. My work space consisted of a few small dressing rooms, a tiny reception area, and the dance studio, about twenty-five by sixty feet. The floor had to be of maple, as all the best dance floors were, and it could never be placed flat against the concrete. It had to be what they called "sprung," laid across a lattice of raised strips of wood so that there was a space between the concrete and the maple floor, to give flexibility. Otherwise, when the dancers landed hard on the floor, they would perhaps break something.

I remember there came a time when we needed a new floor because the wood was too damaged for me to continue my work. At this time I was about eight months behind in my rent, but I went up to Mr. Kaplan fearlessly and said, "I need a new floor. If I don't get it I am moving out. Also, you must treat James, the elevator operator, better."

The new floor was installed, and James got a small raise.

That was the beginning for the special place I have in my heart for anyone named Kaplan. Many years later another Kaplan, Joan Kaplan Davidson, came to my rescue. When we began our company again in the early 1970s, after an unexpected and unwanted lapse when most people turned away, Joan sent the first check. Just recently, when we stood to lose many of the original Noguchi pieces Isamu had made for me, as well as the possible disbanding of the company, Joan stepped forward again. If there is a company now as I write, it is because of Joan Davidson.

The classes were held in the late afternoon and early evening. There was no other way. Most of the girls in my company worked during the day to support themselves. They worked as waitresses, salesgirls, anything they could find. I did not get many girls who were stagestruck. Most came to the dance, turned to it in a way, as an enrichment. They found their way into the arts, into the excitement of life, which was for them a terrific place. These girls turned toward themselves and this led to the dance. They gave up everything to be able to dance.

Many came to me with conventional notions of prettiness and graceful posturing. I wanted them to admire strength. If I could give them only one thing, that would be it. Ugliness, I told them, if given a powerful voice, can be beautiful.

My own company, as it formed, would sometimes come and work with me at six o'clock in the morning and then they would go to their jobs, and return late at night to work with me again. Then as now, dancers did not have an easy time of it. I wonder how many people know that when a dancer is out of work—if there is a layoff, if they cannot teach elsewhere, or if they have no independent incomes—they have to find any work they can to go on living. I have never been able to have my own dancers on a yearly salary. Just once, I would like that to be possible. For as much as they suffer when there is a layoff, I suffer too. It is unfair that dancers don't have more security, don't have a pension program (my dream for my school). For a dancer's life is not a long one. Now that I no longer choreograph on my own body I need them as my canvas and my instru-

"Tragic Holiday" from Chronicle, *December 20, 1936.*

ment. Without them I cannot really work, and for me that presages the
end.

Some of my dancers have been remarkable. Anna Sokolow was filled with
the desire to dance, to move, to create, to enter new areas of life. Her
mother did not approve. She wanted her to earn money, and dance kept
her away from this, away from the sweatshop. But Anna kept doing both
because she was filled with it. Her mother threw her down a flight of
stairs, which crippled her. After this, I went to Anna's mother to try to

buy her out of the sweatshop. Anna did both. She danced with me at night, and worked in the sweatshop during the day.

Sophie Maslow was a working girl, too. Every moment she had she danced. She spent all of her money that way. She was devoted to it and she just loved doing Hanukkah dances, and folk dances about tilling soil and harvesting, which can frankly get a little boring. That, combined with someone telling me that in Hebrew the word *maslow* means "butter," must have lain in my subconscious. Once, when Sophie was particularly off in a section I was trying to teach I yelled at her, "Oh Sophie, you are so agricultural."

Gertrude Shurr came to me a sweet little girl from Brooklyn. Her mother was not too happy that she was dancing, but we had a nice talk and I calmed her down. Gertrude was full of energy, always restless. One day in exasperation in rehearsal I let her have it: "Gertrude, I am thankful for just one thing about you. That you are not twins."

The late class schedule enabled me to have time for myself. If I was working on a new piece I would fix a red ribbon to the door, which signified that no one was to enter the studio. You did not want to be invaded when you were in the holy of holies, which it was when you were trying to create a new dance. I was very nasty and distant from people then and never revealed anything until it was done. And if I had an idea, I wanted it done exactly that way. Everything I do has a reason, a very definite reason. All of these things were very secret to me. I did not reveal them until I was done. There were, however, students who peeked in through the crack of the door.

The school was across the street from the old Schrafft's. Mr. Kaplan, who believed in my abilities as a dancer, was always worried that I was too

With my dachshunds, Allah and Madel, after I injured my knee.

skinny and that I was not eating properly. He used to give Gertrude Shurr a couple of dollars and say, "Take her across the street and get her to eat something." If I had any money it always went back into the dance, either directly for the upkeep of the school or for costumes or to fund a performance.

I had two dachshunds, Allah and Madel, who were very darling and always underfoot. I was teaching and they had to be fed at certain times. There was a woman in the Village, a neighbor, who fed animals at certain times when their owners couldn't. So Allah and Madel were taken to this woman for their supper every night.

During the day, the dachshunds were with me in the studio, in my dressing room. When the bell would sound at the end of class, they would come to the door and look at me. Sometimes they would appear before the class was over, poking their heads into the studio.

"Not yet, not yet," I'd say, and they would turn around and go back into their little beds. When I had my serious knee injury and had to rest on a chaise longue for hours at a time, they would come and jump up on the chaise and place their long bodies across that knee and just sit there in perfect sympathy with me, as if they would heal me with their love and attention, and perhaps to a point they did.

I lived in Greenwich Village, on Ninth Street and Fourth Avenue, in a house owned by Miss Nancy and Miss Loulie Kirkman and Sam Kirkman. You can see it today; it's the second house from the corner. I had the top floor, two small rooms which I tried to keep separate from the daily world of rehearsals—no radio, no telephone, and always sparsely furnished.

Miss Loulie told me that George Washington and some of his prominent guests had had a tea party in one of the neighboring gardens in back. But Miss Loulie said she saw no sense in calling it a tea party when they no doubt served something stronger.

Agnes de Mille lived a few blocks from me in the Village, on Tenth Street. I think that I only let Agnes down once. It was in the 1930s and she wanted me to introduce her as the Dance Debutante of the Year at Carnegie Hall. "Agnes," I said, "you are an individual and I would not presume upon it. I'm not all that much older than you are. How can I do it?" I felt, at the time, that she did not need me in order to enter the dance world. She had her own individual style. She brought her many gifts to the American stage. Her Degas studies, no longer seen, were magnificent. How I wish she would revive them now for the new generations.

We became very good friends and have stayed friends throughout our years. I do not make friends easily but when I do, they are usually forever. Whenever I was in trouble Agnes was there to speak for me and to fight for me. I can never forget her generosity and courage, not just for me, but for herself in her illness and recovery, a great example for others to take hope from.

The Village then was utterly different from what it is today. I was riding through it recently and it was nothing like the Greenwich Village I knew. Then, all of the houses were old and low. Most of the artists lived and worked there. I didn't know many very well because I was too busy working. Most of my time was spent in the studio. Around this time, things in the Village were very intellectual. People would sit around and talk about things constantly. I never really went in for that. If you talk something out, you will never do it. You can spend every evening talking with your friends and colleagues about your dreams, but they will remain just that—dreams. They will never be made manifest—whether in a play, a piece of music, a poem, or a dance. Talk is a privilege and one must deny oneself that privilege. But I never dealt with myself as an artist. I dealt with myself as a person who had an infinite number of details which suddenly demanded to be revealed. I made no effort to be other than what I believed to be honest.

I rarely went to parties, only to concerts, where I searched for new music.

I did Miss Hush from the house on Ninth Street. The March of Dimes had a radio show where people would send in ten cents and they would be dialed in order to give them the opportunity to guess the identity of Miss Hush. It was through John Murray Anderson that I was chosen because of my voice; he said it was sexy. Each Monday I would broadcast a clue all over the country. One was "Dancer, one of the reindeer."

When my identity as Miss Hush was announced, it was early evening and some friends and neighbors began to gather on the stoop. I remember

the owners of the grocery store and the men from the corner shop stood at my door to wish me joy. It was quite a wonderful evening.

Shortly after my time as Miss Hush I was to give a performance, and when I arrived at the theatre the marquee was lit with MISS HUSH WILL APPEAR TONIGHT.

I said, "Miss Hush will not appear tonight, you can take it down. I am Martha Graham and I've been playing the part of Miss Hush, but she will not appear." I told the manager to pack up all of our clothes, but then, of course, the sign came down.

I danced at St. Mark's in the Bowery, a wonderful old church in the East Village set up in the form of an old meeting house. I was in front of the altar rail they had then. I wore a blue dress and I hovered over the crib, which represented the crib of the baby Jesus. The bishop turned to one of his associates and said, "What is she doing?" And he slowly took off all of his insignia, one by one, the collar, the ring, and so on. All this I could see very clearly as I began my dance. Not exactly a strong confidence builder; it just got me mad. After he watched my dance for a while he put them back on. His disapproval of the dance seemed to have ended. He realized I was not going to create a scandal; it was safe to return to being the bishop. I was all right, I guess.

141

I remember when Joseph Buloff took the cross. Buloff was an actor in the Yiddish Theatre who went on to star on Broadway. The first time I went to the Yiddish Theatre it was an unbelievable shock. They acted so wildly and so strongly and I was very taken by it. I would go there often because it was so wonderfully theatrical and Louis Horst liked it.

Buloff was playing a cardinal and he held a cross in his arms which he caressed as a lover. It was very erotic and I was thinking that the cross is a very holy object and that his actions were obscene.

Dancing A Florentine Madonna *at St. Mark's in the Bowery, New York City.*

At my mother's home in Santa Barbara, 1930s.

When I went to visit my mother once in Santa Barbara, we were sitting around the dining room table after supper listening to the radio. It was Maurice Schwartz in a production from the Yiddish Theatre. My mother had no idea what was going on, what she was listening to.

"Martha, what is that language?"

"It's Yiddish and I'm homesick." It reminded me so much of New York.

Maurice Schwartz owned many of the Jewish theatres. For the opening of a new theatre on Second Avenue in 1926, he wanted something completely new, a variety of what were known as modern styles, to be used in one production. For this purpose he chose the play *The Tenth Commandment* by Abraham Goldfaden. Michel Fokine arranged the dances, and Joseph Buloff was first introduced to the American public in this production.

Many times, I'd go with Louis Horst to the Cafe Royal, which was filled with writers, actors, painters, and poets from the Yiddish Theatre as well as from the English-speaking stage. Louis and I would each have a cup of coffee; we had little money for anything else. It was a time of ideas, of conversation, the bringing together of many different kinds of people.

In March 1932 I was granted the first fellowship given to a dancer by the John Simon Guggenheim Memorial Foundation, which offered me the opportunity to go to Europe and study with the German dancer Mary Wigman, but I said no. I didn't want to go to Europe without something American so I chose Mexico as a compromise. Some people still think that I studied with Wigman. But that is not the truth.

I was in Mexico during the agrarian revolution. Men wore very short white pants, white tops, and big hats. They rode in the streets in a wild fashion on any pony they could get. Guns were constantly being fired, but nobody cared enough about my presence to shoot in my direction. I remember climbing to the top of the pyramids. It was so striking going up those steps and arriving at the top to be absorbed in a very hallowed place. I raised my hands high above my head and was enthralled by the wind and the sun, the height. A great deal of what I do today is not only American Indian but also Mexican Indian. It is not that I tried to

143

On top of the Pyramid to the Sun, Mexico, 1932.

be either a Mexican or an Indian, but to gain the ability to identify myself with a culture that wasn't mine. One begins to realize that all human beings are the same.

In December 1932 I appeared with my group on the inaugural program of Radio City Music Hall. The music hall, with its ability to seat six thousand people, billed this evening as "a pageant of the entire theatre" ranging from jazz to grand opera and from circus numbers to dramatic sketches. Harald Kreutzberg was also on the program. Kreutzberg was a concert dancer in Germany. Originally a graphics designer, he began to study with Mary Wigman in Dresden. I remember, during the Second World War, that the dance community joined together to send whatever rations we could to Dresden—food, clothing, anything we could spare, which was not much in those days. Kreutzberg was a solo performer, more or less. Some of his dances were based on Greek mythology, some on literature, but most were formed out of his own ideas and emotions.

During the war, when the American troops occupied Austria, they came to the house of Harald Kreutzberg in Salzburg. A woman answered the door to find an American lieutenant on her steps. Then a man appeared behind her.

"This is my brother," she said, pointing to Harald, who stood at her side.

Harald was recognized as the great dancer he was and the lieutenant turned to his troops and said, "No one will occupy this house. This will be a sacrosanct place and no one will take it." Such was Harald's extraordinary reputation as a dancer.

During the performance at Radio City I was given a nickname after Paavo Nurmi, an Olympic track star from Finland. I was called "the Nurmi" as I ran and ran and ran all around the stage.

I remember there were three times as many Rockettes as members of my company. We had so little room to perform, though the stage was enormous.

We survived opening night as did the other acts, with the near exception of the trained horses; no one could remember where the elevator for the horses was. Samuel Rothafel, "Roxy," whose dream Radio City was, died soon afterward and immediately I received my pink slip. My lawyer told me to report ready for work each evening, so that I could not be fired and would receive my check, which I did. It was the Depression, and I wasn't the only one who headed toward Radio City. Word had spread that there were maternity facilities at the Music Hall in case an expectant mother was to give birth. Hospitals were expensive, and more than a few mothers spent their days waiting to give birth watching the movie and stage show. I often wonder how many Radio City babies there are out there.

For the first few days of rehearsal none of the other acts would even talk with us. I found out later that with our severe movement and costumes they had thought we were all Greek and could speak no English. I tend to think they just thought we were so odd they wanted to give us a wide berth.

Katharine Cornell was, from the 1930s onward, one of the greatest actresses on the American stage. So strong was her following that in each city she toured she had to place this request in the playbill: "Miss Cornell is deeply moved to return to her beloved [Detroit or San Francisco or wherever], but she asks her audience to please not applaud each of her exits and entrances." Katharine was not arrogant when she put that in, just practical. It would have ruined the performance. I remember Katharine as a beautiful woman and a wonderful actress. One day I was watching her rehearse a scene, where she exited rather quietly. I said to her, "When you leave the stage, take everything with you . . . even the piano. Everything. You leave nothing because your presence has been taken away."

One afternoon, Katharine turned to me and said, "Martha, I must play Juliet next year. After next year I will be too old." She was then fifty-five, but onstage she burned very young. Katharine asked me to do the dances for the three or four couples in *Romeo and Juliet*. One person would lead a group of four and then go to the next group of four; it was a constant exchange of movement. Then Romeo would say his line, "Who is she that makes the candles burn bright?" There was one very dark, handsome young man in the group who simply could not get the steps, and keep up. I had to take him out—with great reluctance, he was so beautiful. He went on to become famous in Hollywood. He was Tyrone Power.

I made the gown Katharine wore as Juliet in the balcony scene. The gown that was originally made for her did not suit her at all. Kit and Guthrie McClintic, her husband and theatre director, called me and I went to their home, which overlooked the East River, and we discussed both costuming and the dance. When they needed me, I was there.

Kit had appeared during a dress rehearsal for the balcony scene in an ill-fitting fiery red costume that had been chosen for her by the costume manager. It was completely wrong and the manager yelled from his seat in the audience, "She can't appear in that costume on my stage. It completely breaks the stage."

I turned on him and said, "Yes, if you had done your work, I wouldn't be here."

During *Romeo and Juliet* I got to spend some time around Edith Evans, who was playing the part of the Nurse. I was doing the dances and trying to help out in other areas where I was needed. I became enamored of Miss Evans's portrayal of the Nurse, thinking perhaps of Lizzie and the wonderful childhood she had afforded me. Some chord was struck in my soul. I went up to her during a quiet moment of rehearsal and said, "Would you mind if I asked you one thing. From what point did you take the characterization of the Nurse, or is this too much to ask?"

"Oh no," she said. "I will tell you the exact line. It is 'I think it best you married with the County.' "

At that moment the whole play opened up for me and brought me back to the days of Lizzie and her care over my sisters and me.

. . .

Katharine became a great friend and a great support. In the early 1940s, due to the war and the very nature of the arts, our seasons were unprofitable. Kit organized a tea and through this event raised over $25,000 in contributions to fund the company.

Though Katharine and Guthrie lived on Beekman Place, they also had a home on Martha's Vineyard. It was located between a pond and Nantucket Sound, near the promontories East Chop and West Chop, and it was known as Chip Chop. The first time I arrived there, Katharine opened the door and I stood very still. It was an amazingly beautiful place, inside as well as outside, but what I was feeling was something completely different.

I said to Kit, who was looking a little puzzled by this time, "I feel the presence of Laura Elliot in this house."

"Martha," Kit said. "Yes, she's buried in the garden."

I didn't know this at the time, had no idea that Laura Elliot, a singer who taught at the Neighborhood Playhouse, had ever been to Martha's Vineyard. But it has always seemed to me that, even as a child, I have been aware of unseen things around me, a certain sense of that movement. I don't know what to call them, sense beings perhaps, or spirits, or a kind of energy that stimulates the globe. There's even a presence that I can feel walking through my home. I know that something exists there. We don't recognize each other, but we are of the same ilk, of the same world.

It was through Katharine that I met Helen Keller, who could not speak, see, or hear. Her speech was difficult to understand for those who did not know her. She was granted the ability to perceive life through her own unique awareness. She was a great lady, and very funny, too. She was, perhaps, the most gallant woman I have ever known.

With Helen Keller and her companion, Robert Helpmann of the Royal Ballet, and Guthrie McClintic.

Helen used to come to my school at 66 Fifth Avenue. She felt as if she was watching the dancing. What she was focusing on were the feet on the floor and the direction of the voices. She could not see the dance but was able to allow its vibrations to leave the floor and enter her body. She said to me once, in that funny voice of hers, "Martha, what is jumping? I don't understand."

I put Merce Cunningham, then a member of my company, at the barre, and placed Helen's hands on Merce's waist.

"Merce," I said, "Be very careful. I'm putting Helen's hands on your body."

Merce jumped in the air in first position while Helen's hands stayed on his body. Everyone in the studio was focused on this event, this movement. Her hands rose and fell as Merce did. Her expression changed from curiosity to one of joy. You could see the enthusiasm rise in her face as she threw her arms up in the air and exclaimed, "How like thought. How like the mind it is."

We would go to the opera and concerts and she would rest her hands on the seat in front of her to catch the vibrations of the sound.

149

Celebrating the joy of dance with Helen Keller in my studio.

One time we were in an automobile together and Helen had her dog Elo on her lap, as we all took a bumpy ride uptown. Helen unfolded her hands from Elo and placed them on my lips so that she would be able to tell if I was speaking or not.

During the start of a meal, she would put her fingers on the table to feel the place setting. She never touched the pieces again except when she needed one. She created a mental picture of what was in front of her. Once we were invited to supper and as we sat at the table, Helen's hands went over the setting, so that she knew where everything was. When she touched the water goblet her hands flew up in delight and she cried, "Oh, crystal!" Her table manners were impeccable, as was everything she did in her gracious embrace of life. But at what tragic price did she achieve that grace?

One of the first excitements Helen felt was running water on her hand. One of the first words she ever understood was the word "and"—"And open the window." "And close the door." It always began with the word "and." "And one, two, three. And . . ."

I think this is one of the reasons she liked to come to the dance, as th_____ from the dance, and leads us into most of th_____ led her into the life of vibration. And her li_____ close the circle, all of our dance classes b_____ "And . . . one."

What I did not permit in the studio was any discussion of politics or religion. There was a time for that, and a place, too. Late in 1935, I received an invitation to dance with my company at the International Dance Festival that was part of the 1936 Olympic Games to be held in Berlin. The invitation was signed by Rudolf Laban, president of the Deutsche Tanz-bühne, by the president of the organization committee of the Eleventh Olympic Games, and by the Reichminister of Volksaufklärung und Propaganda—Dr. Joseph Goebbels. Actually, before the formal invitation arrived I received a call from the German Embassy in Washington. I was asked if I owned a shortwave radio because a message beamed directly to me from Berlin would come the next day. I went to Barbara Morgan, a wonderful photographer who collaborated with me on a book, to hear the message read by Goebbels. He said that when the borders of Europe were one for all time another great celebration would be held in Germany, but for now the great artists of the world would join with each other in Germany, and my name was read. The formal invitation arrived, late in 1935. It never entered my mind even for a second to say yes. How could I dance in Nazi Germany? I replied:

"I would find it impossible to dance in Germany at the present time. So many artists whom I respect and admire have been persecuted, have been deprived of the right to work for ridiculous and unsatisfactory reasons, that I should consider it impossible to identify myself, by accepting the invitation, with the regime that has made such things possible.

"In addition, some of my concert group would not be welcomed in Germany. They are Jewish." When I was told they would be perfectly immune, I said, "And do you think I would ask them to go?" The Germans said in that case they would ask an inferior dance company to represent the United States. I said, "Do. But just remember this: I hold the official invitation and I will publish it across the country to show that Germany had to take second best." No American dance company went to the festival. After the war in Berlin, I was found on a list of those to be "taken care of" when Germany controlled the United States. I took it as a great compliment. And when I later performed in Berlin's new Philharmonic Hall, I took my solo about a triumphant biblical Jewish heroine, Judith, with a score by a Jewish composer, William Schuman.

Saint-John Perse had to flee his homeland during the war. He was a great man, a great poet, and a strong influence in my life. He was born in Guadeloupe as Marie-René-Auguste-Alexis Saint-Léger Léger, lived in

France, and barely escaped from Paris during the German occupation. The Gestapo immediately ransacked his apartment upon the arrival of the Nazis in Paris but he was able to leave for England, and then the United States.

He was in the United States as a diplomat. He told me that I could use any words or lines from his poetry for my dance. The inspiration for my 1973 dance *Mendicants of Evening* came from St. John Perse's poem "Chronique." Marian Seldes, a gifted actress, spoke the lines, and moved very much like a dancer. It is a poem about experiences of later life, and a life well lived. "Great age, behold us," Perse wrote, "take the measure of man's heart."

Though the war was not fought in our country, many Japanese-American citizens were placed in internment camps. One of my dancers, Yuriko, came to me shortly after being released from one of these camps, and has been with me ever since. Today she holds the title of regisseur, and is director of the Martha Graham Ensemble, our group of advanced and professional-level students.

Overseas, in Spain, the tragedy of the Civil War brought immediate response from artists. We all chose to respond to the horror of it in our

Deep Song, *December 19, 1937.*

own way. I chose *Deep Song* (in Spanish, "Cante Junto"). It was a solo piece like *Lamentation,* but here I used the bench in a more active way. The bare stage opened to me in my black and white striped paneled dress, while Henry Cowell's music began to play. This was in December 1937. The following year, with Anna Sokolow, Helen Tamaris, Hanya Holm, and Ballet Caravan, we performed in a benefit to aid the democratic cause in Spain.

In 1937, I danced at the White House for the first time for President and Mrs. Roosevelt; I would dance there for seven other presidents. I danced in a little garden that was filled with flowers. There was a young man who was in charge of looking after me who said, "You will not go and meet the President of the United States barefoot."

He said this to me so many times that I finally replied, "My bare feet are part of my costume. I do not go barefoot in my own house. I would never appear before the President of the United States barefooted."

Eleanor Roosevelt and I became good friends during the 1940s. Once we went to a United Jewish Appeal meeting that was being picketed by Orthodox Jews. They were picketing against men and women sharing the same swimming pool. They wanted men to have it one day and women the next. Our car was stopped by the picket line. Finally Mrs. Roosevelt said, "I've had enough of this. We are going through."

She was sure that she was right. I thought, Oh my God—for me to walk through a picket line at this time in my career will ruin me.

She said, "Martha, come with me."

And Martha came.

Mrs. Roosevelt invited Marian Anderson to sing in Constitution Hall, but was refused by the Daughters of the American Revolution. I told my mother, who was a member, that she had to resign. She said, "Oh really, must I, Martha? They give such nice parties." I gave up then and there with Mother. It was hopeless.

Tragic Holiday, *December 20, 1936.*

I told her, "Don't bother your head, someone else can resign." And she didn't.

Shortly after, Marian Anderson was denied admittance to the Algonquin Hotel, in New York. She had engaged a suite for herself, but the management did not realize she was black until she arrived. Then they were terribly apologetic, but nonetheless said that the suite had been taken and she could not have it. When I found this out I was furious and went right up to the manager at the front desk and said, "Very well, I won't come back to the Algonquin, either."

So I packed up my baggage and left the hotel. I could not stay. It went against my grain.

When I went to see President Truman I did not have the proper dress. It was an evening dress but it wasn't very beautiful. Several women had been invited to meet the President and to each he gave a picture of himself. He turned to me and whispered in my ear.

Well, when the press saw the President whispering to me, they rose to their feet and tried to find out just exactly what it was he had said to me. "Why did he speak to you? Why did he talk to you in that way?" I did not answer. But what he said wasn't at all controversial. All he said was, "If you return later, I will give you my autograph."

About this time I went to a dinner party given by Emily Genauer, critic of the *New York Herald Tribune*. There were a lot of unfamiliar faces, but then suddenly one man stood out from the rest across the room. It was Marc Chagall. I did not go up to him immediately. I was a nobody at this time, just part of a group enamored of his work.

Gradually, we came face to face, and I said, "It seems to me that every animal that you draw or floating creature that you paint is built on your own face. You are to me the animal."

He was quiet for a moment or so and then he kissed me and gently slapped my face. "Little one," he said, "you know too much."

·   ·   ·

MARTHA GRAHAM

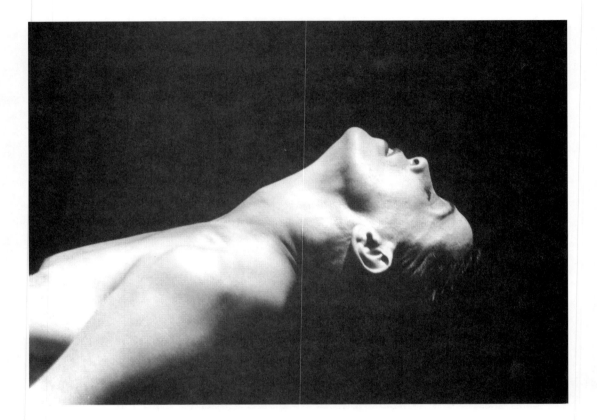

Photographs by Imogen
Cunningham, Santa Barbara,
California, 1931.

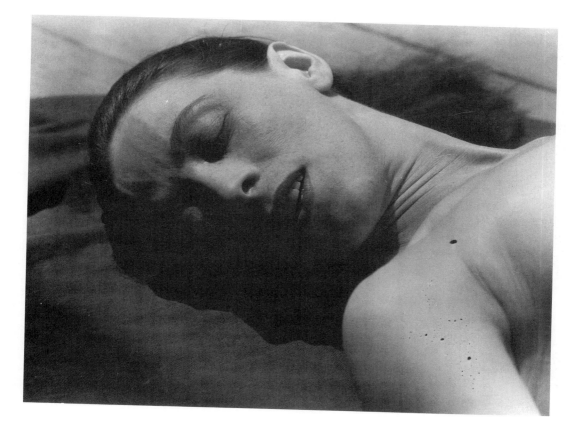

Men in all walks of life have sustained me. I treasure them in every way. Many have made marks on my life. I like men. I adore men. Many have adored me.

In the early days when I still had an active night life I wouldn't be caught dead in bed without a light makeup. But I was never promiscuous. I always had only one boyfriend at a time. I didn't have time for lovers or love affairs—with some delightful exceptions. My philosophy of lovers and boyfriends? When I loved them I loved them. When I didn't, I left. That simple. And I suppose I wasn't always that nice at times.

All of my life I have been a devotee of sex, in the right sense of the word. Fulfillment, as opposed to procreation, or I would have had children. I chose not to have children for the simple reason that I felt I could never give a child the caring upbringing which I had had as a child. I couldn't control being a dancer. I knew I had to choose between a child and dance, and I chose dance.

No wonder the Graham girls were always considered a little fast in Santa Barbara, though not by today's standards, of course. It's funny to think of the difference in morals and attitude between then and now. I had so little knowledge of life and sex—my mother taught me absolutely nothing. Once I went with my Aunt Re and her second husband to San Francisco. We walked all over the city, up and down the hills, from the waterfront to Chinatown. Suddenly, I noticed a woman on a street corner. My aunt walked between me and this woman.

"Who is she?" I asked Aunt Re and her husband.

"Martha, she is a soiled dove," he told me. I had no idea what he meant. When I returned to Santa Barbara I asked my mother about the soiled dove. She nearly fainted. Everything was very conservative in Santa Barbara. My mother was horrified and would not discuss it.

One relationship that became a love affair was with a sensitive, extraordinarily handsome artist in California, Carlos Dyer. Merle Armitage and

Ramiel McGehee were two men who were friends of mine from California. Merle was an author of books on art and theatre in America. Ramiel's background was a little more mysterious, although he was a Zen master and reputed to have held a post with the Japanese emperor in Tokyo in the 1930s.

Both Ramiel and Merle had what I guess you would call a crush on Carlos, who was absolutely heterosexual. Merle decided to ask me out to California ostensibly to work on a book about my attitudes toward dance. Carlos would be invited to do the illustrations. They were absolutely sure we would have an affair that would break up Carlos's marriage, and knowing I probably wouldn't stay too long with him, they planned to pick up the pieces of Carlos's life for themselves. The plan worked to a point. I have heard stories that it was love at first sight for both of us, that we disappeared to a guest room at Merle's house, had our meals sent up, and didn't emerge for several days. This is absolutely untrue. I would never behave like that as a guest in someone's home. Carlos and I went to my beach house.

To add to the complications, Ramiel began to work with me as a Zen master. Each day he left me a koan to reason on, to brood on, to find my way. Through him I learned as much as anyone can ever learn about Zen. This knowledge served me in good stead, in terms of self-discipline and clarity of focus, and simple, pragmatic behavior, no matter what Ramiel's motives were in taking me on as a student. I suspect they were not free of self-interest.

My relationship with Carlos was a glorious one for me physically and intellectually, and I know he took it very hard when I decided to leave and return to New York. He wrote me the most beautiful love letter. I don't believe in looking back, yet ever so often I am tempted to read old love letters, but I don't.

.   .   .

With my friend and musical director Louis Horst near Cricket Hill, Bennington.

In 1934, I began to teach summers at Bennington College in Vermont, a wonderful place where we were given the freedom and possibility to make our dances. There were artists there throughout the season, including Doris Humphrey, Charles Weidman, and Louis Horst. Once, in one of Buck-minster Fuller's geodesic domed houses Louis was too big for the shower, a triangular one that he had persuaded Buckminster Fuller to build in the first place. At this time, he weighed about three hundred pounds and could not get himself out. Louis hated being constrained in any way. He was very frightened, with good reason, because it took a couple of people to pull him out.

I would blissfully drive around the campus and the town in a little model-T Ford, with no license, and no fear. But Martha Hill, who founded the dance program at Bennington, lived in terror of the trips. When I took other teachers for a drive, she would say, "Pray! With Martha's driving, that could be the end of the history of modern dance."

Jean Erdman, a dancer in my company, was there with her husband, Joseph Campbell. They had met when she was his student at Sarah Lawrence. Their families objected to their marriage, because of the age difference, yet they had one of the most perfect marriages I have ever seen. Joe was a luminous being in all of our lives, one who opened gates to mysteries past through his knowledge and insight into the myths and legends that touch all civilizations. His intuitive soul and spirit guided him and us through these gates, on journeys of discovery. He enabled us to treasure and to use the past and to recognize the blood memory within each of us. I have so often said that dance should illuminate the landscape of man's soul, and in my journey through that landscape Joe was a profound influence.

It was Jean who first spoke the poetry of Emily Dickinson in my ballet *Letter to the World.* I conceived of two Emilys, dressed alike in white, who opened the ballet, each one entering from the opposite side of the stage. Throughout the dance the Emily who spoke would witness the other Emily, myself, who danced the inner landscapes of the poetry. The first lines as we faced each other were, "I'm nobody! Who are you? Are you nobody, too? Then there's a pair of us . . ."

For the first performance in Washington, D.C., before we did the actual afternoon rehearsal, Jean went to each of the three stage mikes at the foot of the curtain and tested them, to what she thought was an empty auditorium. "I am nobody!" she said to the first two mikes. At her third "I am nobody!" a little boy who had been hiding behind a seat apparently couldn't take it anymore, and jumped up to call out, "Lady, you got to be somebody!"

The first performance in New York could have had a disastrous end. I had no idea that you had to have permission in order to use Emily Dickinson's poetry, from her literary executor, Martha Dickinson Bianchi, a woman with a fierce reputation, fully capable of standing up during the performance and stopping it. She was there that night. When I learned she was coming backstage, I dropped my dressing table mirror. Not a good sign. She swept in all in black with black jet beads and an almost dead-white face, looked at me, and said, "Young lady, I have no criticism, and from me that is high praise." And she left.

When I received the news that Joseph Campbell had died in 1987, I sent to Jean my words of sympathy and I recalled to her lines of Emily Dickinson that she had read in *Letter:*

> *After great pain, a formal feeling comes*
> *The nerves sit ceremonious, like tombs*
>
> . . .
>
> *The feet, mechanical, go round*
>
> . . .
>
> *A wooden way*
>
> . . .
>
> *This is the hour of lead.*

One other gift from Joe I couldn't believe: in the opening program of his television series, "The Power of Myth," he showed film clips of individuals who were key to our civilization: Gandhi, Martin Luther King, Mother Teresa—and a clip of me dancing *Lamentation*. I could not believe it when I saw it.

Hunter Johnson composed the music for *Letter to the World,* which we premiered in Bennington on August 11, 1940. John Martin of the *New York Times,* usually a strong supporter of my work, wrote, "Better to let it slumber in the hills of Vermont." But from that initial debut to its revised presentation the ballet changed, as did Mr. Martin's opinion. In some ways I couldn't blame his harsh criticism; it did have some elements that bordered on kitsch or perhaps went beyond it. One was the Faerie Queen I devised, who entered on point carrying a bird cage with a little stuffed bird in it. The others I shudder to mention, so I won't.

When Hunter saw *Letter to the World* again in the early 1970s he wrote me to say there was a curious change from the original. The first time he saw it the ballet was fifty minutes, and this time it was fifty-eight! That, I said to the dancers, is what is the matter with this dance. What we have to do is bring it back to the way it was composed. We did it, with screaming and mayhem on the part of some of the dancers. We removed the slack, the leeway. We brought it back.

Eric Fromm was at Bennington, as well as the poets Ben Belitt and William Carlos Williams. Ben's poetry more than once animated me to work on a ballet. There is that wonderful phrase of his, "Acrobats of God." What is an Acrobat of God? I feel it is a person, not necessarily a dancer, who lives fully and completely. It is taking your chances whether you fall or not.

My 1947 ballet *Errand into the Maze* owed its title and its thrust in some ways to Ben's poem of the same name, published in his book, *Wilderness Stair*:

> *The errand into the maze*
> *Emblem, the heel's blow upon space*
> *Speak of the need and order of the dancer's will*
> *But the dance is still.*

The title of my dance *American Document*, which premiered in Bennington on August 6, 1938, came from the poetry of William Carlos Williams. Dr. Williams was a general practitioner in Rutherford, New Jersey, and he permitted me to use his name, his words, anything I wanted. We were all experimenting, and permitted each other certain liberties. He gave me a great deal.

Alexander Calder had a primitive and startling idea about space and the uses of the stage. Calder's pieces moved. He designed the pieces for my ballet *Panorama,* which premiered in Bennington in 1935. The next year, for *Horizons,* he created a set of mobiles and stabiles, which had to be manipulated from the sides, by two dancers. This was new for the dance and we wanted to make clear to the audience the role of the dancers as opposed to the role of the set. We placed the following in the program notes:

"The 'mobiles' designed by Alexander Calder are a new conscious use of space. They are employed in *Horizons* as visual preludes to the dances in this suite. The dances do not interpret the 'mobiles' nor do the 'mobiles' interpret the dances. They are employed to enlarge the sense of horizon."

Calder did sketches of my dancers and he wrote a note saying, "Martha, if these don't seem right to you, let me know, and I'll try again." He had that much humility.

Sandy Calder came to Bennington in his old automobile with Feathers, his French sheepdog. According to Bennington lore, when he emerged from his car, he was wearing nothing but his undershorts. He was taken immediately to a rather conservative men's shop in town to be outfitted.

"I need some pants," Calder said to the salesman.

"You most certainly do," came the reply.

That was in the 1930s. A few years ago we had a young man working for us who came forth with some strange news before we left for a tour of Europe. He said that he knew a private collector with a Calder set he was willing to sell. He would give some of the proceeds to my company, as long as the sale was done anonymously. Fair enough, we thought. The collector's lawyer met with my lawyer. It sounded like a miracle. We went off to Europe.

There I received a call from Sotheby's. They said, "As you know, we have accepted this Calder that was made for Martha Graham without any of the usual documentation because Martha Graham's word is good enough for us, but can you please tell us when you replaced the original ropes with wires?"

I was puzzled and asked Sotheby's to check the catalog, which stated, "From the collection of Martha Graham."

The young man knew we were going to be in Europe for six weeks and had used our stationery to confirm ownership. Sotheby's sent us a photograph; it wasn't my Calder at all. I had the picture sent to Bonnie Bird and Gertrude Shurr, who had danced in the ballet in the thirties. They called me and said, "Martha, this is not it."

That verified that. It seemed that the young man had made it himself, so Sotheby's took it out of their catalog.

More recently, I learned that someone else was trying to buy that same fake work. People think that they can get away with anything. They try to, at least. I loved that Calder. I felt that it had the spirit of Calder, the man who made it. I have no idea where it is today. I did not give it away.

I had a little cottage in Connecticut, very charming and very small. It was wonderful to be able to leave the city and drive into a different landscape. Sandy met me there once to show me new things he was working on.

After we had looked for a while, Sandy decided he wanted to display some of the smaller objects. He attached a wire from one tree near the cottage to one closer to the road. He began to hang his mobiles from this wire. They were like unknown birds of the imagination in all of their colors and metals, which came from another world to land here.

It didn't take long for us to realize that we had an audience. The cottage was alongside a highway and suddenly the traffic backed up. People wanted to see what was happening, what these odd shapes were. Some cars pulled over to the side of the road and people gawked at the mobiles and at us. We could see people shading their eyes from the sun to look into Sandy's now brightly lit work. They had never seen a Calder before. They just thought the two of us were off our rockers.

At the Perls Galleries with Alexander Calder.

Back in New York, he invited me to his gallery, the Perls Galleries, and said that he wanted me to have something, anything I wanted. There were three things that I liked very much, which I made note of when we walked around the gallery together.

"Martha," he said, "you can have all three."

Well, the other people in the gallery, especially the owners, Dolly and Klaus, looked as if they were about to die. I chose one, a gouache, which I look at every day as it hangs in my living room. It was so like that special loving, playful side of Sandy, floating balloons and tulips. He also used to make the most wonderful jewelry for his friends, and he gave me a hairpin, which I still have.

· · ·

Betty Ford was a student of mine at Bennington in the 1940s, when she was known as Betty Bloomer. She is still a very dear friend of mine, dear in the sense that we understand each other. When she comes to my apartment there are usually five guards—two downstairs at the elevator, two outside the door to my apartment, and one young man who sits with us as we talk and records everything we say. We have no privacy at all, but that is part of her life as a former First Lady.

President Ford presented me with the Medal of Freedom, the United States' highest civilian honor, in October 1976. This marked me, as the Japanese mark their artists, as a National Treasure, while marking the first time that the medal had been awarded to a dancer and choreographer. Frances Steloff came with me to the dinner—Frances, who had signed a

Receiving the Medal of Freedom from President Gerald R. Ford in 1976.

loan for my first concert in 1926 and without whom there would have been no award ceremony that night. President Ford came right up to Frances, put his arms around her, and said, "Frances, you made a good investment."

Years later, in the 1980s, Betty went to Washington to speak for me to Congress about an appropriation we needed so desperately. She worked tirelessly for it. But then, she is my friend and she would stand by me. The weekly or so telephone conversations we have, which are usually very long as we chat about everything from trivia to philosophy, are a beacon of light and friendship for me. Another example of what Emily Dickinson meant by "an act of light."

With Erick at Bennington College.

While I was teaching at Bennington, Lincoln Kirstein, director of the Ballet Caravan, suggested that Erick Hawkins study with me. Erick became the first male dancer in my company, and later, my husband. Before Erick, there were no men in my company. Mothers and fathers did not want their sons to be dancers. They thought it was effeminate and not a very pretty thing to watch. Only when men became heroes—strong, gifted-body men, as I think they are in my company—only then did we have men. And Erick was the first.

First let me say something about Lincoln. The first time I met him was after a performance of *The Cradle Will Rock*, in 1937, by Project 891 of the Federal Theatre under the direction of John Houseman; Orson Welles produced. This production in the years between the Depression and the Second World War took a controversial look at labor troubles in Steeltown, U.S.A. This period of theatre, with John Houseman working and his brilliant protégé Orson Welles lighting up the stage, has been seldom equaled in its intensity and creativity. I knew John from the early days when he and his wife Zita Johann (the princess Ananka in Boris Karloff's film *The Mummy*) lived at 66 Fifth Avenue. He directed my film, *A Dancer's World*, and served as chairman of our board for a good long time. After the performance, as my companion and I were walking through the lobby, Lincoln and I were introduced by a mutual friend. He said, "I admire your dance."

171

I replied, "Well, that isn't what you recently wrote. You called me the goddess who belched and I have never forgotten that."

He said, "But that was before I knew you."

I said, "You don't know me now." And walked away. And that was that.

Erick and I were in Santa Fe, at K. D. Wells's house, on September 20, 1948. It was just after the March of Dimes period when I had danced at the White House, alone. That morning he came into my room and said, "You're going to get married today."

I said, "I'm not. I don't want to be married." I cannot say whether within myself it was vanity or whether it was the desire to keep my own name. In any event, we got into the car, drove into Santa Fe and were married by a Presbyterian minister in the foyer of his church. There were no witnesses except the minister's wife and another person who just happened to be there. I had only one dress that I could possibly be seen in. It was a black taffeta skirt and coat specked with red. I had created this little arrangement, which I thought very handsome. I wore a little veil over my face. Erick couldn't resist looking over my shoulder to see what age I would put down, but I was consistent. I took off the same fifteen years that I always had. After all, Ernst Kulka, my wonderful Viennese

Demonstrating a lift with Erick.

Rehearsing Every Soul Is a Circus *on the lawn at Bennington
with Erick, right, and John Butler.*

doctor, had said I could get away with it, and as a doctor's daughter I knew better than not to follow my physician's instruction.

Erick danced with my company, and gradually we had a very deep love affair. After eight years of living together, Erick decided we should marry. I didn't want to but I did it. During that ninth year it all fell apart. It shows. Never try to hold on to anything.

After we were married we got into the car and drove to a nearby Indian pueblo, and our life started there. I kept my own name; I was determined to use it. I did not want to be the wife of anybody if I had to give up my own name. After our first night together as man and wife we awoke, and Erick turned to me and said, "At last I'm free of this terrible thing." I had no idea what he meant then, and I didn't want to know. I only knew that I loved Erick very much, not only physically, but also as a companion. And we were very happy, as Eugene O'Neill put it in *Long Day's Journey into Night,* "for a little while, until things became difficult." I remember an evening back in New York when I, in desperation, went to the Lady Chapel at St. Patrick's Cathedral. As I was entering to pray, I saw Celeste Holm leaving. Our eyes met, and all she said was, "You too?"

I would hardly call myself an outdoor girl, but I was so in love that when Erick wanted to go camping in the Grand Canyon I didn't hesitate. I even cooked in a fire, made in a mound of earth I had scooped out. I still remember the food; corn, steak, and potatoes. As evening fell, Erick and I each slept in our own sleeping bag. Later in the evening I awoke and felt a presence, something strange near me. I looked up and saw a tremendous Navaho woman on a horse gazing down at me. Her red skirt rested over the horse's rump. We looked at each other for a short time

Then go on as one who has long life
Go on as one who is happy
Go with blessings before you
Go with blessings behind you
Go with blessings below you
Go with blessings above you
Go with blessings around you
Go with blessings in your speech
Go with happiness and long life
Go mysteriously.

　　　　—Hopi prayer
　　　　　American Document
　　　　　Premiere, April 6, 1938

and then she rode off, as quietly and as mysteriously as she had arrived.

I remember going to Gallup, New Mexico, with Erick and seeing the beautiful handwoven Indian rugs. These were sacred rugs; one part of the rug is left incomplete, and usually some small flaw is included in the design. It gives the rug a sense of being, an act of becoming. It is made more beautiful and more mysterious by what is left out.

The American Indian dances remained with me always, just like those haunting moments before sunrise in the pueblos, or my first view of the Hopi women in their squash blossom hair arrangements that I was to use in *Appalachian Spring*.

Erick was very much caught up in the whole idea of Indian culture. Although I have been greatly exposed to the Native American tribes, I have never done an Indian dance. I've never done any ethnic dance. I've received an excitement and a blessing and a wonderment from the Indians.

My times in the pueblo, though, were always times of discovery. I saw a woman there who held her baby in her lap while she was sitting on the ground. The baby was between her legs and he wasn't walking yet. She was manipulating his feet in the way that their dancers manipulate their feet. When this child grew older he would not have to learn the dance. He would already know it. It would have become a part of his memory and entered the rhythm of his blood.

El Penitente is a dance of the Penitentes of the Southwest, a sect which believes in purification from sin through severe penance. Even today, the sect practices its ancient rites, though they are banned by the Catholic Church as unholy acts. I saw a woman in a pueblo walk on her bare knees over cactus leaves, as the rites were performed. *El Penitente* is presented in the manner of the old traveling shows. Isamu Noguchi designed the original set, including a screen, which covered over the girl—Virgin, Magdalen, Mother—when she had committed the crime, the seduction of the penitent.

The penitent would chastise himself with cactus leaves, thrusting them on himself to show God that he had been wicked, had fallen in love with the girl. She enticed him with the apple, the apple that is her virginity. At one moment in the dance the priest is dressed like a god in a big black coat. The penitent falls, is brought to his knees in contrition by this creature, and his face is slapped by the holy man.

In the original production, Erick was the Penitent and Merce Cunningham, the Christ figure. A few years ago, Misha Baryshnikov danced the role of the Penitent in a gala performance. He took the role so completely to himself that his back was absolutely red from the rope of flagellation.

The last time I went through the Zuni pueblo I witnessed the ceremony called the Shaliko. During this dance the Shalikos, joined by the Koyemshi, went into people's homes and disarrayed them if they thought some evil had taken up residence, or if there was a suspicion of practiced witchcraft. They were almost like policemen.

Taos was a beautiful part of America with a unique landscape. One of the Taos Indians married the heiress Mabel Dodge Luhan. The marriage did not go very well. Mabel had bought him out of his first marriage, from the tribe. Someone asked him if he had ceased loving her. He said, "I will not divorce her. I have disgraced my tribe enough by marrying her."

Mary Austin was a writer in Santa Fe who identified herself very much with the Indians. She became a heroine to one of the Indian tribes. One day a flute was stolen, one that was sacred to the customs and religion of the Indian people. It was Mary who searched furiously for that flute, and discovered that it had been sold to a museum outside of Santa Fe. She was instrumental in getting the American government to return it to the tribe. She would come to the pueblo and the chief of the Indians would stand and cry, "Mary comes, Mary comes." The cry would be constant, would fade away in the pueblo and rise up again as she entered.

I remember one night I was outside the pueblo on a hilltop. Across from me, the Indians were seated on their own hilltop. It was a cool night with a moon that enabled both our hills to be lit. After the ceremony of that night you could not go into the pueblo. They had laid cornmeal at the entrance to the tribal area, which meant that Indian business was afoot and you could not enter. Cornmeal was the sign to stay away and this was to be obeyed until the cornmeal was removed.

The Navahos have a bridal necklace of beautiful stones. I have one which I wear quite often. The groom gives this to the bride and he also gives his mother-in-law a pair of bells, which she is to wear so that he will know when she is approaching.

There is a Navaho chant I will always remember: "Beauty lies before me, beauty lies to the right of me, beauty lies to the left of me. I walk in beauty. I am beauty."

A tremendous argument broke out between Erick and me. When he left the house, I called Mrs. Wickes, my analyst and then his, using one of those old-fashioned phones attached to the wall. I asked if I could see her.

Mrs. Wickes was a wonderful woman. She and I became friends, and I would go to have a drink or supper

When Cris Alexander was to photograph me in 1950 after my separation from Erick, I wore branches in my hair that I had found on the street.

Erick and I greet new students in the dance studio at Bennington.

with her. She told me that after sessions with some patients she had to open all the windows and doors to air out her room. She once lectured me on arrogance and said, "Martha, you are not a goddess, you must admit your mortality."

Erick had asked her if she could make him a better dancer and choreographer than I was. Mrs. Wickes said, "No, I cannot." Frances Wickes did not vibrate to that sort of request. Erick said, "Therefore I break my analysis." And he walked out, not only from analysis, but gradually, from our marriage as well.

One time the company and I were dancing in New York. Erick gave a performance of his ballet *Stephen Acrobat*. At this time, he was not receiving favorable reviews. The audience had booed his performance and he had retired to his dressing room. I was so anxious to join him and comfort him. But Charles Chaplin came backstage with his ravishing young wife, Oona O'Neill. He told me that I had used my body as a tragical instrument. Not even this compliment could take my mind off joining poor Erick. I stayed and listened to Chaplin and it was hypnotic, yet I remember silently saying to myself, I will stand by Erick, even if it means I must leave New York. As much as I wanted to talk to the Chaplins, I knew that Erick needed me and I excused myself from the conversation to be with my husband. But I will always remember that evening, the childlike gleam in Chaplin's eyes, and the sense of play in his body movement.

Erick insisted that we go to Europe. He felt that it was the only place where he could be reviewed well, as back home the reviewers were prejudiced in favor of me. He did not want to be judged in the shadow of my reputation in America.

My interest was not in Europe, and in some curious way, I feared it. I can still remember the exact moment in Paris in *Every Soul Is a Circus* when my injury came. Erick and I were center stage; I was doing a simple plié and my knee went. I whispered to Erick that I was badly injured, to help me, and we got through to the end. But by the time the curtain came down my knee was the size of a grapefruit. It was a gala event at the Champs Élysées Theatre, with Mrs. Roosevelt in attendance, and somehow I got through the reception. But it was agony.

It soon became clear that I could not complete the Paris season. Doctor after doctor wanted to operate on my knee. At that time, in the 1950s, that usually meant the end of your dancing career and so I waited. All through it Bethsabée de Rothschild, a former student, was a dear and very supportive friend. She was also the sponsor of the engagement. We never would have been able to afford it had she not helped. Bethsabée was even the author of a book on American dance, *La Danse artistique aux U.S.A.*

The company moved on to London, and more doctors. We were

Punch and the Judy, *August 10, 1941. From left to right: Jean Erdman, Ethel Butler, Jane Dudley, me, Erick, David Zellmer, David Campbell, Mark Ryder, Merce Cunningham, and Pearl Lang.*

Just before I tapped Erick with the flower in Every Soul Is a Circus, *I thought,
"Where did you come from? I could eat you up." December 27, 1939.*

hopeful of at least saving the London season. When it became clear that it, too, would have to be canceled, Erick left me. He divided our money, left a note, and was gone. I was crippled and very much alone but for Bethsabée. I went back to Paris with her and stayed at the Avenue Foch home of the Rothschilds. It was a terrible time, and I had to find a way out.

One afternoon Bethsabée asked me what I would like to do. I suggested going to see the Rothschild Bank. She looked at me as if it was a very odd request, but we went. When we arrived I was amazed. It was unlike any bank I had ever seen. No real tellers, no depositors that I could see. "Bethsabée, where are the depositors?" "Depositors?" Bethsabée had evidently never been asked that question before. "We don't really encourage depositors, but yes, we do have one now . . . the Pope."

During my stay at Avenue Foch, Bethsabée shared the story of how the Rothschilds fled Paris before the Nazis entered the city. They had little warning and arranged to drive to Nice and take a seaplane to Lisbon, then a boat to New York City. Seaplanes evidently look a lot safer and steadier than they really are. Each member of the family could take only a very small suitcase for the journey. Bethsabée described how she looked around her bedroom deciding what to take and said, "Oh, Martha. I had the most beautiful Vermeer by my bed table. It would have fit in my suitcase, and I started to pack it and then I put it back. I realized if I took one thing like that I would miss all the rest." When they reached Nice, they were short one ticket for the seaplane. Bethsabée's father had to buy it from a passenger. I always wondered what he must have been willing to pay for that one ticket which would save his daughter's life.

It soon became time to move on, to return home and face the school and the company and my injury. Erick wanted a divorce, a Mexican divorce. I contributed to it because he wanted it, but it shattered me.

I finally decided to return to Santa Fe. The Southwest always had a healing, nurturing effect on me. I stayed again at K. D. Wells's home, one of the most beautiful in Santa Fe. There I found a very old doctor who was able to help me through careful use of weights and exercises done at the same moment each day, a very well thought-out regimen. I started lifting very small weights. I got to the point where I could put a typewriter in a sling and lift it with my leg. When I was able to lift twenty-five pounds, I was healed. With his help and being in New Mexico I think it all came together for me, because I recovered to the point where I could appear at Carnegie Hall and do my twenty-minute solo, *Judith*. As I made up for the performance, there came a knock at the door. It was Erick. He said, "I will come back and escort you home at the end." I didn't answer. It was a very bad thing for him to have done. The performance was a success. I had gotten through. But after all the visitors who came backstage had left, Erick knocked. I waited and almost didn't want to answer. When I saw him I said I would go home alone. And I did.

Erick and I had had a love affair, a very deep love affair. I never loved anybody but Erick in that way. It was difficult to get over it, but what choice did I have? I remember the first New Year's Eve we were not together. I resolved to put on my beautiful Chanel to look my best and to go to the four parties I had been invited to. I remember sitting in a taxi en route to a party, alone, hearing the New Year come in as a clock somewhere in the Village struck the hour. At that time the open, unplanned new year was a terrible landscape for me to contemplate, but I had to go into it.

The clearest picture I have of that time are in my letters to my analyst and friend, Mrs. Frances Wickes.

New London, Conn.
July 16, 1951

Dear Mrs. Wickes:

I wish I could have seen you those few days. I did not leave New York until Saturday afternoon. There were so many things I managed to leave until the last and they had to be done. I think I had not really planned to leave at all in my deep heart . . . not for anyplace, California, Connecticut or Maine. At the end I found it almost impossible to leave although in my mind I thought I had been looking forward to it. Sometimes it seems as though this would never end and yet it must in some way or I shall end.

My first day of teaching is over. I enjoy teaching even though the classes here are too large for anything except the most elementary attempt at communication. There were about 60 in the class today . . . in each class I should say. They move well but there is such an emptiness of meaning or real intention . . . it is a kind of bleakness of spirit where there should be some urgency and deep foundation of meaning no matter how faulty the technic may be. There seems to be a desire to dance, to move well, even to say something with it but there seems to be no glimpse of the primary reason why dance is or why it has to be done or why they are doing what they are doing . . . there is such a fundamental waste of livingness at the root of it all and that should be the root if anything is. Perhaps I expect too much but it seems they start with the result of dancing rather than the cause. All I can do in these five days is to make them a little more aware through shock and an attempt at building and progression. But then again it will be a painful experience if they get it at all and perhaps it is better and kinder to let them sleep as they are now . . . to employ what I call the "rocking chair" method of dancing . . . comfortable, rhythmic, monotonous, safe . . . Perhaps they should never leave the chair to stir those depths of the shadowy pool near which they rock their lives away.

I think I never want them to be on fire if it is so painful for them as it is for me. I wonder how long one can stay on fire. It is a curious fire. Perhaps it is good for Joan. I wonder. At least I think I know what it does mean to burn slowly from within . . . to feel so possessed by flame as to be infinitely hot and about to disintegrate into an ash at any instant. It may be very beautiful to watch. People here speak of my radiance, that I look as though I had found a new life . . . Perhaps it is the final glow and not a beginning.

Tomorrow is July 17th. It will be one year since London. I keep thinking some special thing will happen tomorrow. I suppose it is neurotic

*Barbara Morgan took these portraits
of Erick and me at Bennington.*

that the day should assume such proportions to me. But I still keep hoping that there will be some sign. I keep thinking that something will happen tomorrow. Of course I always think it might be Erick. There is one thing which does frighten me in all this. That is the fact that the despair seems greater than at any given time in all this year. I feel in some way it should lessen but it does not. Or at least that I should become sane and reasonable about this, more so than I was a few months ago. But time only seems to intensify the feeling, it seems. I remember a woman who killed herself in Santa Fe last summer. It was on the seventh anniversary of her son's death. I thought it strange even then that she had been able to endure those years and then had succumbed. Now I think I understand the increasingness of despair. Time seems only to serve as a crucible wherein fire intensifies the contents to its essence and the result is a quick and earnest poison utterly pure and incorrupt in its action.

The month of June was an accumulation of intensity. At least it served to show me one important thing . . . that I was far from free and that I was still engulfed in hoping. We had a party one Saturday, the last of the June Course. Erick was there. All went well. Then he asked if he might watch my class the next day. He did. And said how beautiful it was. Then he came next day and asked to watch again. Then he sent me a note and a book of Cummings poems, saying it was the most beautiful thing except Judith and that the last poem made him think of Judith because for him it was the most beautiful poem in the world. Those are little refinements of an exquisite torture even though not intended as such by him. He would be shocked if I told him that. I did one thing when I thanked him for the book . . . it was foolish of me but it could not be helped. It was the last day and I was tired and lost a little. I asked him if he wanted me to get a divorce this summer as I had not planned to do it unless he wanted it. I know why I said it. I wanted to touch him, to hurt him, to have some personal contact with him. It was weak and stupid. I did not become at all emotional although I said I loved him still. He said yes, that he knew that and that I need not get the divorce, but to let things solve themselves as they would. You see how damnably deep this is and how tenacious the roots are even when there is no soil to cling to or draw nourishment from.

I am not a very satisfactory patient. I am self-willed and stubborn. I have only done one outgoing thing. I had an idea for a dance and I wrote to Virgil Thompson, asking him if he would consider doing the music. I did not send him the script because he may be involved or unsympathetic. It is not *The Scarlet Letter*. I did not want to fit myself into another woman's life again at this point although I may return to that. This is one night. It has a working title . . . *Point of the Wolves*, or *Promontory of the Wolves*. I think of Point Lobos and those lovely twisted trees. It is a night or a year or a lifetime . . . but it is crisis and the wolves are the hungry ones who tear at the heart with that cruel hunger that only wolves have.

It would involve the company but it is essentially about one woman and her tide-pool at night where driftwood and dead things float after the surge up of the sea. There is a sequence . . . Storm at dark, moon-rise and moon-set, deep dark and dawn. With my mind I add the dawn. I know there must be a dawn but as yet I have no sensation or knowledge of it. But it is logical that dawn comes. There is a luminous bathed essence of new day. Perhaps if I live through the progression up to that instant I shall capture some of the lovely instant pervasive green which marks the return to color and life which is dawn. Perhaps I have not yet reached the instant of deep dark which precedes the dawn. I may be still living with the curious strange fantasies of the moon world, the images beautiful and terrifying but less so than the reality of the actual which would release me into the lovely anonymity which is dawn.

It sounds vague. It is and yet it is not.

Have you seen the book . . . *The Sea Around Us* . . . by Rachel Carson? I am beginning it. I think it is important. It is a scientific book and yet it has all the mystery and magical sense of first things that poetry has. Even the titles of the chapters read a little like a journey each of us takes . . . The first part is called Mother Sea. Then the chapters:

The grey beginnings
The pattern of the surface
The changing year
The sunless sea

The hidden lands
The long snowfall
The birth of an island
The shape of ancient seas.

While it is scientific it might be read as a fever chart of any evolution . . . human or a world in formation . . . and the points of arrival are those which mark the journey of the heart in experience as well. Perhaps I am going back to the images you spoke of. I cannot say. Some of this is frightening. It is so utterly alone. I fight that aloneness and the slow way life has of moving far below the surface in its warm breeding zone . . . all is change and dying . . . and slowly meeting the demands of environment and change. There is a merging of forms into other forms at shocking cost of life energies of all kinds. It is all implacable and serene and ruthless and consuming and utterly smiling always because time has no terrors to that which refuses to recognize time. Its only definition is its own agency of progressions. It is the Shiva dance. There is that eternal dancing with the ceaseless smile and the ceaseless implacable pulse of no time which is at one the death of time.

If you will let me write to you occasionally and let it fall by the side of your heart so as not to disturb you or eat into your thought and infinitely important activity of self-being of you, then I will write. But it needs no reply. I am just dancing something I cannot explain yet. My hair is wild and I hear nothing. Or perhaps if I do it is the pulse of a heart I am afraid of. Perhaps I am seeking by certain destructive ways of experimentation to find the heartbeat.

Yesterday I went to the beach after I arrived here. It was hot and quite lovely and the sea even though it is a sound has a magic. It was a private beach where little mobile islands of families floated. I sat for hours. I watched and waited. It was for some kind of sign I think. It tore into me in a way. Then I knew that I had always joked a little about my next incarnation and that I should be a dancer again . . . a ballet dancer and do *Swan Lake*. But I knew yesterday that was not it . . . that I would have children. I think I could never say that before. I never could release myself to become the most simple and elemental instrument of life . . . I had to be in control or govern even against nature . . . or else I wanted to be three parts god like Gilgamesh. . . .

I had hoped the summer would bring you the peace and fun and work you desire and need. It has done me good to speak to you. . . .

Martha

Santa Fe, New Mexico
August 26, 1951

Dear Mrs. Wickes:

Your letter was wonderful. I have read it many times. I knew my absorption with the wolves or with the idea of death was perverse in some way or at least let me say the part of the truth rather than the picture of it even in my own mind. There have been some very bad days, especially here. That was inevitable, because I am still so stubborn. I suppose some of the tenacity which has made me able to hang on to my work at times when there seemed nothing to permit me to hang on to has made a character trait of tenacity, and it makes it part of all the behaviour, including this matter of Erick. I let go with reluctance if at all.

Craig Barton came for a week. I think I told you of him. He went to Europe with us in a managerial capacity. It was about Craig I thought of when we talked of the dream I had when I awoke hearing myself say . . . "I must go south before I go west." This was the first time Craig, Lee and Bethsabée and I had been together since we were in London on That Night. I thought in some way I had reached to the ultimate of that experience but I found here that I had not. There were several things I had still refused to face and part of it was my behaviour. So by talking gradually in between times when we went on picnics and saw Indian Dances I found out several things. One night it all seemed too much and I wept. It terrified Craig as it usually does certain men who are unable to cope with a woman in her elemental period of destruction. But after a few days of pressure it has settled into place where I can see it as an inevitable part of the picture I have to put together. The men left a week ago.

In the usual way there have been parties here and it has been pleasant. We go to Los Alamos tomorrow for dinner. That is always strange and divided in its impact. The antagonism against it here is great and that part is inevitable. But there is also another aspect to it I feel certain. That can be constructive. It has seemed to me that a struggle between good and evil in an allegorical sense is taking place and it needs both to produce one absolute, or perhaps I mean an absolute. There may have been days here when we did nothing except to lie by the swimming pool. We are in a kind of cottage hotel where we do most of our own cooking. That freedom is pleasant. But there have also been days when it has seemed all very useless and without pattern for a future.

I have not written the letter to Erick. It means I have to be able to tear myself up for once and all and I have avoided the performance. But the time when I can do it is approaching. Curious revealments take place . . . some dreams of disturbance and some incidents which I have read a certain way even though it may be wrong. There is one I should like to tell you about.

Craig had an Indian boy in his company in Karachi. He was from the Cocheti pueblo which is near here. Craig wanted to see him and so we hunted him up. He has married and we found him working in a G.I. school of carpentry. He has two little boys, one a year old. The one named Matthew, the one-year-old one, was born with a heart malformation. It does not function as it should so they have had to have him in the hospital here with the operation facing them. Just so far can José . . . the father . . . understand. So Craig endeavored to explain it to him. It meant we went to the Indian Hospital here. The aftermath I need not tell you because we were able to partly convince José, we think, that the authorities were doing all for the best and we saw the doctor in charge. But the point of all this is something else.

In the hospital there was a baby girl of six months whom they said was up for adoption. The child had been there since she was born. I saw her and she was lovely . . . not all Indian, I believe. I told Bethsabée about her and then ideas started. I found myself thinking of this child, thinking seriously of what it would mean to adopt her. Bethsabée said she would give me money. I cannot say that I ever entertained the idea with all sincerity, but there was some thought of it in my mind as a fantasy sticks sometimes. One night I lay in bed thinking and in some moment between sleeping and waking she became a curious reality. I saw her with me in the future. I saw myself walking with her . . . I even saw her name and heard myself accept her. Her name is Sandra. I did not know that at the time so I named her . . . Ericka. I suppose it was startling to me because it is the most vivid reality I have had regarding a child, the most complete identification of my life with one of a child's. Of course nothing came of it. I asked about her and found out the conditions of her birth but even before that I knew I only wanted to help her find a home if money was needed because I knew Bethsabée would give it.

Now I think I have reached another phase of the dance I am thinking of. It is a continuation of the *Point of the Wolves* of which I told you. I had been thinking of the Cypress Tree . . . the Cedar of Lebanon of which you had spoken, and I knew that image of constancy in the face of the elements was also deep within me. There were two bad days when I was caught in a deep negativism. It was partly the fact of the place and partly that Craig had left. But I am glad I came here this summer. It has made it another place, not only the place where I was married. It has a beauty of its own and it will have for me a life of its own separate from the memory of that experience.

In the middle of a desperate moment I stood in the middle of the room here, trying to fight through the negative darkness. I flung out my arms and said, "Why not call this new dance . . . I salute my love" . . . Then I knew I was arriving someplace even though the title or the idea may never be right. It has seemed to move again . . . the idea. Perhaps it will take the form of writing it out . . . it could even be the letter that I must write to Erick someday even though he may never see it. It has not made me unhappy, or sentimental, I believe. And it seems to be falling into the same pattern in a way as the wolves but in a very different way . . . .

Twilight . . . which is like a sarabande of recognition

Moon-rise
Moon-full
Moon-set

which is the evocation of memory deliberately and
precisely done with no sense of tragedy.

Deep Dark
which is like a dark miracle where all is excluded
except the absolute of the struggle

I would hope that if it can be done without embarrassment of unnecessary
revealment that it could become a work. It might be that the personal
would be absorbed in the impersonality of the experience as a life pattern.
There would be no duets and no lover would appear any time throughout.
At this moment the struggle is no longer with him but with myself to
accept the principle of lover rather than concrete.

All this is in a state of evolving. It helps me to speak of it to you and
if you do not mind I am grateful. Something is coming out. It may not
be what I think I want and I may think yet and do what I want, to be
swept back into a more warm and simple way of living . . . this in no way
takes care of any state of the future other than it may make a path for me
to walk on to meet the future, whatever that is to be. Perhaps the need
to project it forth in terms I can understand, dancing or stage work, the
pattern of so many years, is needed. I know I run great danger in this
subject. I think it is not in danger as far as I am concerned of being a
sentimental wail . . . at least so I think. I think it is some necessity to
transmute a sentimental experience into something constructive and perhaps creative.

I had been to the House of the Navajo religion here. There was one
large reproduction of a sand painting with great bands of color across the
whole of it, running from north to south with the usual opening on the
east. The colors were:

white
black
grey
yellow

in that order. The custodian told me the significance of the colors in the Navajo sense. I forget exactly but I mean to find out before I leave. It has to do with directions and with times of year. Then when we went to the Frijoles canyon I saw there a series of earth formations in the museum telling of the different layers in the volcanic land or in the activity of the volcano, and the colors were exactly the same as the sand painting. All this you know in your infinite simple and deeply wise acceptance and recognition of life. But I tell of an experience to me, that is all.

This has been a long letter, longer than I have planned. I have not spoken of Erick and a letter I had before I left New York. But that has little or no bearing on any of this. I cannot even say how much bearing it has on me at all except that I have not been able to erase certain things from my thinking by the simple and complex means of supplanting them entirely by something else. I know this is all very opposite from suppression. I know from my dreams that I seem still to be caught up in a resentment. But this facing of London anew and with a degree more of entirety helps to release my sense of guilt to me so that I can in time release it from the absorbing memory which is vanity. But if there can be in some sense an erasure of the sense of lasting mistake, then it will be good. This last is a little mixed.

I hope you have had some time of beauty and fruitfulness. I am certain you have had. But still I worry a little about you in perhaps a presumptuous way. But I like to think it is because I treasure you. Your hand is on my life.

Martha

Mission Inn
Santa Barbara, Calif.
August 1, 1952

Dear Mrs. Wickes:

I had promised Katharine Cornell I would go to the Vineyard for a few days and I did. This has been my time for missing trains. Beginning with Connecticut I have missed every one except one out here. I have been here since Sunday and spent one day in bed with a slight upset stomach but now begin to look better . . . at least I do not have those deep furrows all over my face . . . I mean more than usual at least. My Mother and sister are well. Mother is tyrannical, of course, in her love but that is nothing new or unexpected. It does come with shock, of course, because one forgets. But it can be coped with. I shall go to Santa Fe for 10 days and that will be a nice return to that potent land. Then there is a composer in San Francisco whom I want to see about a new piece. I know I should vegetate and perhaps I can when I let down a little more. It takes time.

This is a curious, lacerating time in many ways. There may be more despair in a certain way, if a complete or, let us say, "completer" facement of facts means despair. The trip across the country was not easy this time. It was just as beautiful but it caught me up into memories and deep longings. The awareness just seems to cut deeper and the great longing just seems to get greater. But at least I know it has to be born and that no kicking or histrionic behaviour will bring ease or escape from it. There will be some other way in time after this has run its course to the depths. I think I am beginning to know what you told me of the acceptance of certain facts . . . the living in or with sorrow . . . and the difference. It is not a question of escape from it, I see, but how it is used and faced. I just may be stuck with this. But I have much company of heart over the world.

I should like to tell you one thing on the good side because this sounds dire. I am not dire. I may be stuck or think I am but not that I am in the misery I was even at this time last year. The only real difference is that now there seems to be no hope. I cannot even say that there is none. Hope is a corrupting, corroding thing. It is, I suppose, a thing of the personal will. Faith seems an acceptance of a larger view of things and a less accented personal attitude. Faith is necessary and hope is not. I suppose it is the acceptance of the larger pattern which is faith that establishes one in that condition of grace no matter what the despair or the misery. I suppose grace can never arrive if hope is there, specific hope. You see, my dear one, this dies hard in me. Or will it ever die?

Martha

El Mirason Hotel
Santa Barbara, CA
August 30, 1953

Dear Mrs. Wickes:

It has been a nice summer. I have resisted and have done a few things. But I am beginning to need to get away. There is a curious need about the summer and I have not been able to achieve it except with Erick. It is that thing of not having anyone look at you. Do you know what I mean? I know you do. It is necessary here to play a part, even with my Mother. Not that it is unpleasant but it means I have to be having a hard time being a woman. I really seem to be having a hard time being a woman. It could be that I go about it the wrong way. We shall see about it. Perhaps I am the vain one who has to be fed all the time but I think I would like to be anonymous for this time. That sounds pompous, I know. But I trust you to find me out no matter how hard I try to evade you.

Always,

Martha

Hotel Des Indes
Holland
March 28, 1954

Dear Mrs. Wickes:

I am reading a wonderful book. It has meant a great deal to me. The only time I have is the few moments of orientation at night before I sleep. It is the new book of Alan Watts . . . *Myth and Ritual in Christianity*. It is quite wonderful for me, and I am at last beginning to understand *Dark Meadow* a little and to know where it came from. That is fun. Oh, I am so grateful to everything that brought me to your door and into the sacred oasis of that room. Everything is worth that for me even though at times everything is slightly lost because I am lonely. Not in one way but in another. It has been a vast and small pleasure to be looked at as a woman and appraised as a woman here in Holland.

Always,

Martha

It is amazing what the spirit can get through if you are determined enough. I still can't believe how after we had separated, Erick and I still had to dance together in performance. Whether it was a dance of consuming jealousy, I Medea and he Jason, or one of tender love like *Appalachian Spring,* he the Husbandman, I the Bride, it came so close to real life that at times it made me ill.

It wasn't until years after I had relinquished a ballet that I could bear to watch someone else dance it. I believe in never looking back, never indulging in nostalgia, or reminiscing. Yet how can you avoid it when you look onstage and see a dancer made up to look as you did thirty years ago, dancing a ballet you created with someone you were then deeply in love with, your husband? I think that is a circle of hell Dante omitted.

There was never anyone after Erick. Perhaps I was wrong. Perhaps there should have been. But there was not. There was no one. Not in any way, passing or significant.

There are a few lines I wrote in my journal shortly after Erick left:

I know it was the bite
of these wide empty, hungry hours
that now devour me, beloved,
when I sometimes caught your sleeve.

My company and I did a State Department tour to the Orient in 1954. We performed in major cities in Japan, Indonesia, India, Pakistan, Iran, and Israel. Before we left people kept saying to me, "But how will they understand your dances? Will you be upset if the audience does not understand?"

Dark Meadow, *with Erick, January 23, 1946.*

I said, "I am not interested whether they understand or not. I am only interested if they feel it." And it's on that basis that I've tried to reveal—through women, through whatever means I had available—the quickening of people's sensitivity, the opening of doors that have not been opened before.

The first time we danced in Italy, in Florence, we had quite a scandal. The audience was out of its mind. They were not used to seeing dance in quite the manner that we were presenting it. At that time, they were expecting dancers who would perform on pointe. And of course our feet, for the most part, were bare.

We were on stage doing *Dark Meadow,* named for Plato's Dark Meadow of Ate. I did not think that this was the piece to bring to Italy, but people told me otherwise and I was finally persuaded. "It's exactly what they want in Italy," they said. "And such a beautiful title."

The audience did not throw things, although I expected something to fly from the first seats onto the stage. But their disapproval was so un-relenting that I turned sharply and abruptly to them to make a gesture. I raised my hand and the audience stopped. In my hand was the ability to halt their behavior; one movement. I said to them under my breath, "You can be had. I'll take you."

The next time the audience misbehaved, I repeated the gesture. The audience again responded. The last time I did it the curtain came down and I said to everybody on stage, "No one bows this evening. No one. Keep your eyes on the floor and stand perfectly still."

The curtain was raised for our bow, but we did nothing. Everybody was still and there was a great gasp from the audience. No bows. Curtain down.

And then a burst of loud applause from the audience. Curtain up. No bows. Curtain down.

This kept going on for quite some time. Finally, during a quiet moment

At Castel Gandolfo before an audience with the Pope, August 1984.

from the audience, I walked to the front of the stage, turned my back on the audience and bowed to my company. Quietly I said to the curtain man, "That is it. No more." And that was it.

This was the first of six performances in Florence. I had no trouble from then on. It delights me to think that years later the city of Florence gave me a beautiful gold medal made from a Leonardo daVinci mold.

In 1984, after an especially successful performance in Rimini where thousands of people had to be turned away, I had an audience with Pope John Paul II at his summer residence, Castel Gandolfo.

I was taken there by automobile. We called ahead to make sure there would be a room for me to change from my travel clothes to my long black velvet Halston gown and cape, to cover my head. I did not want to meet the Pope in a wrinkled dress.

I was taken into a rather ornate room, when suddenly the Pope came walking toward me. All that he said was, "You're Marta."

I said, "Yes, I'm Marta."

He gave me a rosary. After my audience I watched him sing songs with children from different cultures of the world, in their native languages, Czech, Polish, Italian.

When I returned from Castel Gandolfo, I ran into Swifty Lazar at the Grand Hotel. Swifty knows a great many famous people and is not exactly shy about sharing that information. Naturally, he asked me where I had spent the afternoon. I was still wearing my black dress.

"With the Pope," I answered. For once, Swifty was speechless.

In Karachi, Pakistan, I used my hand in an entirely different, instinctive, way than I had in Florence. We had just performed and were invited to a reception by the head of the museum. I was one of the last to arrive after removing my makeup and costume. I entered a great, long room filled with people, but what caught my eye immediately was a bird on a perch across the room. It was a falcon, a bird I had never seen before. I had never seen the stance of a falcon during a falcon hunt, and I don't think I had ever read about it. I don't know what induced me, but I placed my left arm in front of me, and the falcon, who was neither chained nor hooded, flew across the room in what seemed an effortless grace of flight,

With Pope John Paul II after the company's performance in Rimini.

stilling the people below him. He came to me and landed instinctively and gently on my bare arm. I wore no sleeves. For a few moments we just looked at each other and there was a recognition.

Think for a moment of the hand. There are a great many wonders about the hand. Think of the handshake between two strangers. It shows "I bear no weapons, my hands are clear. I will not hurt you." That is why it's such a phenomenon and so nice to see people clasp hands.

In Burma, after doing *Cave of the Heart,* I was given a nickname which translates into "Elephant Going Amok." What we call the "cave turn" comes from this dance, from fifth position. You turn to one side. As you keep turning to one side more and more your leg comes off the floor and you make a wide turn.

One of my first nights in Burma I had a dream of a lioness that padded across my room, beckoning me to follow as it left through the wide-open doors.

In Rangoon we danced on a teakwood stage, constructed for the occasion on the grounds of the Schwedagon Pagoda. Upholstered furniture from all over Rangoon was hauled out to the field in front of the stage. There, many of the audience cooked their meals, and I could smell the most marvelous curries while I danced Medea. Of course, I could not eat before a performance, but looked forward to a nice hot curry, one of my favorites, when I finished. For five nights, four to five thousand people attended the performances. I remember, during the day of an evening performance, I was taken to a local community school where a charming young boy danced for me while I sat at his small desk. Throughout the tour, the natives of each land gave to me the gift of their culture through the presentation of native dances. In the evening I tried to do the same.

I have in my apartment today a bed that I found in Malaysia. I saw it while we were driving around on the back roads of the country. The bed is a thing of beauty, of terror, a work of art. All of the symbols on it are wonderful. They said it was an opium bed, a little bed a person lay on while he was taking opium. But this particular bed is a bed to sleep on. It has two drawers in it—one contains all the medals I have received and one contains odds and ends, from one glove to a pin missing a clasp that is just about to be repaired. Each piece has a different meaning for me. They are not just objects, but things that have contributed to me in one way or another.

I love jade and have a few pieces of it in my apartment. One of my favorites is a pi, a round, flat piece of jade that an emperor used to call out to the gods for a propitious harvest at the Temple of Heaven in the Forbidden City in Peking. Jade, to me, feels like the voice of the gods. It is beautiful, whether it is an object, an animal, an archaic piece, or the pi.

With Jim Thomson's beautiful cockatoo in his home in Thailand.

Jade is beautiful and assumes a shape, which was part of the conversation with the gods.

When we performed in India, Nehru came backstage to see us. He was so human and approachable. He brought us flowers and was surrounded by many children. When we spoke, we were surrounded by his security people. Forty-five years later I was asked to a reception his daughter Indira Gandhi was giving for a group of women in New York. I hesitated about going. I plagued my friends with my doubts. "Why," I said, "she won't even know who I am."

I entered a long room filled with many people. When I walked through,

Indira Gandhi left the others and came up to me and looked deeply and simply into my eyes.

"Don't you remember me?" she asked. "My father took me to see you dance in New Delhi so many years ago."

I remember visiting Mahatma Gandhi's tomb. It was filled with many flowers and people stood completely still. There was a banyan tree, an enormous tree that becomes several trees. The roots come down from the tree to the earth to make another tree, another legacy, another forest.

Nehru was quite a different man from the Nizam of Hyderabad, for whom my sister Geordie and other Denishawn dancers performed on their tour of Asia in the 1920s. While they danced onstage, he left his grand throne and walked through the performers. He touched the fabric of their costumes, while they continued to dance. At the end of the performance, he greeted each of them and had his man walk behind him, holding a gold chest encrusted with emeralds and rubies. He was then the richest man in the world. Geordie told me all the dancers were so eager about the prospect of the gift he would give to each of them. The box was slowly opened and the first gift was presented: an orange.

On my last visit to Israel my friend from the early days, the mayor of Jerusalem, Teddy Kollek, would come and visit me at my hotel on the Mount of Olives and we would watch the sunset, the great drama of those sunsets—the blazing sun, and suddenly, violently, it was gone. One afternoon I gave Teddy a very old piece of jade, thin and delicate, a dragon biting its own tail. He gave me a lovely piece of blue Roman glass, a coin with a woman's head on it. I later found it was an entry coin to a bordello in ancient Jerusalem.

I had worked with Bethsabée de Rothschild in 1964 to train the Batsheva Dance Company, Israel's first modern dance company, and later, for a time, I gave them some of my works to perform. In the beginning I was

Moshe Dayan was very proud of this 10,000-year-old stone mask which he is showing me in the garden of his home in Tel Aviv.

not hopeful of much success. The girls dressed so heavily, many in army uniform. No theatricality, I thought. But one day in the dressing room I watched, and under their daywear they had the most lovely lingerie, and I knew it would be all right. "You dress to undress," I told them.

Bethsabée was my first patroness and she was with us in the Middle East. She had been a student of mine downtown when I had no idea who she was. Her father was a descendant of one of five brothers who went from the ghetto, in Frankfurt, to become the bankers to the world.

Bethsabée joined us as my wardrobe woman because she had to appear on the program as something, so she was listed as a wardrobe woman. And that is what she became. I said to her, "I have never had a wardrobe woman who wore Dior and smoked Dunhill cigarettes."

And she was an excellent wardrobe mistress because she would not allow a wrinkle. Not one wrinkle! At that time, Middle Eastern women had no ironing boards. They only had cushions and ironed everything on them. When an ironing board came over with my company the Egyptian people had a fury fit, because they just went so crazy to have to iron on a board when all those years it had been done on a cushion.

I was brought up on stories of the Egyptians. I remember the stories of the magic of the river. In Egypt my room was near the Nile and from my room I could see the Nile in all its beauty and all its wonderment. It always seemed to me to be so filled with animals. It had such a life to it, that even today I can look at the East River near my home and see that Nile, as if it flowed to me now from that part of the world, as if it were at my reach.

I created the dance *Phaedra* in 1962. We were in Germany when New York Congresswoman Edna Kelley went to Washington to protest our being sent overseas on a cultural exchange program. She went so far as to suggest that some form of censorship be imposed on all of the art forms that were being exported from America. Another Representative, Peter J. Freylinghuysen, agreed with Mrs. Kelley. He described *Phaedra* as a dance with a lot of couches and young men in loincloths. "We couldn't quite make it out," he told the newspapers, "but the import was quite clear."

And so in Brussels I had to hold a press conference in order to assure the United States government that I was not doing something to embarrass the country. *Phaedra* was too sexual, I was told. One senator, who walked out of the performance, took the microphone and asked me how it felt to be an ambassador representing my country through eroticism.

"I have always thought 'eroticism' to be a beautiful word," I answered. Back home, the dance community was very supportive, as were most people involved in the arts. Even today, there is always someone with an eye toward censorship. It all starts again—Jesse Helms is not a new phenomenon.

As far as sex is concerned, I think that it is quite beautiful. I do not know what life would be without it. I don't believe in nude dancing on the stage. To me that is a bore. There is a certain beauty about sex that can only be expressed through eroticism. I like the beauty of the body and I enjoy what it expresses about life. For that reason I don't deny sex. I have had no reason to. I've only glorified in the beauty of it. Only hidden things are obscene.

I think that censorship is the height of vanity. There have been people who have done nothing but try to censor my work. I learned to say nothing. This is the way I see something; you don't have to look at it if you do not wish.

I know my dances and technique are considered deeply sexual, but I pride myself in placing onstage what most people hide in their deepest thoughts. Emily Dickinson in her own proper way said that all of us have moments "when shy humiliations gambol on sunny afternoons, who is to say not to do it." The artist is simply reflecting his time. He is not ahead of his time; it is the audience for the most part that must catch up.

It bemuses me that my school in New York has been called "the House of the Pelvic Truth," because so much of the movement comes from a pelvic thrust, or because I tell a student "you are simply not moving your vagina." It led one company member to tell me that when I coached one of my ballets, *Diversion of Angels,* at Juilliard for their graduation, he came away thinking that the Martha Graham Dance Company was the one dance company in America where the men suffered from vagina envy.

All of this has to do with eroticism; it has nothing to do with the late-night blue channel on cable television. Absolutely nothing.

Not that my frank descriptions haven't gotten me into more than a little trouble. On our first tour of Asia, in Tokyo, one of my dancers had wandered off with several American sailors and was nowhere to be found

Clytemnestra *with Bertram Ross, 1961.*

for the matinee performance. After we left the theatre I turned to a friend in the taxi we hailed and said, "She never would have been a great dancer. She doesn't move from her vagina." The Japanese taxi driver nearly swerved off the road. "You understand English?" I asked. He turned and smiled, "Yes, ma'am. I was raised in Brooklyn."

Night Journey, my 1947 ballet, is a dance between Jocasta and Oedipus, mother and son. It is a highly erotic dance. I have never believed in the necessity of interpreting either music or story in dance. I believe in writing a script of movement or a musician writing a script of music. Two can join and they do join. For Jocasta, I saw beyond the time when we discover her on the stage.

Jocasta is standing at the foot of the bed with silken cords raised high in her hands. Before that moment I sensed her wandering the columned halls in a frantic fury to reach the great doors. These Grecian doors were sculpted in the most beautiful way: tall and identified with momentous happenings. Jocasta opens the doors, into this chamber of her life, and closes them behind her. We find her standing at the foot of her bed with the cords raised high. The cords are silken cords, identifiable with the umbilical cord. The great sin of incest will dominate her later life. She had unwittingly met the young man who in time she accepted as her lover and her husband and as the father of her children. She did not realize until a great while later that she had committed the crime of incest, that she had married her own son. Her life of love and motherhood was spent in this sacred room. I would like to believe that she was born in this room: perhaps she was, perhaps she wasn't. Her love life was consummated here. The birth of her children occurred here. And she rushed here to meet the final destiny of her life, her suicide. She carried in her hands the umbilical cord which was to her finally the symbol of her crime against civilization and life. But as she is about to slip the cord over her head to be strangled, Tiresias sounds his wooden staff on the floor and it wakes her to a consciousness of his demand that she relive her past in its entirety before she can be permitted the peace and the forgetfulness of death.

Tiresias comes forward with his staff and rips the uplifted cord from her hands and throws it on the bed. She falls, and the furies rush in. Those furies, the daughters of the night, are the terrors we all have. They are memories of things we dread to remember, things we wish to forget— the terrors. They must be recognized and lived through until they leave your mind.

213

Now Jocasta kneels on the floor at the foot of the bed and then she rises with her leg held close to her breast and to her head, and her foot way beyond her head, her body open in a deep contraction. I call this the vaginal cry; it is the cry from her vagina. It is either the cry for her lover, her husband, or the cry for her children. The dance proceeds but there are small intimacies that I have never revealed in words. All of these things mean a tremendous amount to me. I don't talk about them much because people might think I am a little cuckoo. But as other people took over the dance it seemed necessary to explain the certain small mysteries that animate the instant in the reliving of the tale.

One of these is when Jocasta falls to the floor, then rises to rush wildly about the stage, throwing herself on her hands, on the bed. She then sinks to the floor, driving to get under the bed, trying to hide from the knowledge that is too much for her. She tries to crawl under the bed. She cannot. She puts one leg up and gets in the bed and rolls to the woman's side of the bed. She turns to lift her robe, and lays it across her as though she were revealing her shame, as though she were naked.

She seeks to veil that shame. Oedipus then enters her life and she finally receives him. He carries her to the stool where she becomes the queen. He dances for her and she rises. Now it is here that I would take three or four steps to encircle the stool, make a wide extension forward, and then three little steps back in hesitancy. Then another wide extension forward and then three little steps back in hesitancy. She does that but on the third time she falls to her feet.

She has in her hands the branches that Oedipus had given her when he carried her from the bed onto her small stool where she became the queen. She drops into a wide split fall and puts one flower out tentatively toward him, sits back and crosses her knees, opening and closing, opening and closing. It is this that a dancer sometimes avoids, hesitating to realize that she is inviting him into the privacy of her body. He comes forward, takes his cloak, and puts it around her. He picks up the flower and the two proceed to the bed. It is this moment of invitation that is sometimes lacking in the dance. Not every dancer can master this moment. It is not only a movement, but rather a gesture of invitation for him to come between her legs. There's another moment, perhaps there are several, where that intimacy, that mystery, is forgotten. The first one was when she covered herself with her robe to veil her nakedness. The second one is when she comes back with him under his cloak to the bed.

There is another moment of privacy. It is when, as her young husband, he seems to lie across her knees as though she were rocking him, and she hears in her imagination a baby cry. She does hear that cry; it enters from her soul. It is the cry of her lover as he subjects her to his wishes. It is the cry of a baby for its mother. They walk forward in another moment; the two of them come straight forward, a very simple walk. I keep thinking of that as the marriage procession where the man and the woman ac-knowledge to the world their great commitment, which is that of the king and the queen.

And then the mystery opens at its end when he realizes that he has committed the terrible sin of incest. She is lying on the bed. He rips the jewel from her dress and with it, he blinds himself. Blinds himself so that never again will he see her beauty or see her to desire her, and he staggers off.

And here again is another little moment of mystery. She rises, she turns to the bed in an all-enveloping gesture, almost a farewell. She turns and proceeds to the front of the stage. Oedipus has taken the umbilical cord and in his violence and his anger against the gods for permitting such a situation, has thrown it from him before he staggers to commit the act of blinding himself. She progresses slowly—perhaps three or four feet. It depends on where the cord lies, where Oedipus has thrown it. During that passage she takes very small steps, very empty steps, as she unfastens her robe in the back. And at a certain moment, maybe three steps or four steps, varying on the necessity, she drops the robe in front of her. All of her queenliness, all of her majesty goes down with that robe.

She steps across it, over to the rope that becomes the umbilical cord, raises it, stretches it out in her hands, looks at it with deep love, not hatred, but pity, affection, and the tragic awareness of what beauty and anguish it has brought her. She looks to the right side of the world—there are buttercups there. The sky has clouds. She looks to the left side—perhaps there are daffodils, the world is inflamed with the beauty of the flowers. It is flamed with her love of life. It is then, in this moment of smiling recognition that the umbilical cord is going to be her savior, her companion, her reason or the evidence for her passage into the world of death, of forgetfulness where memory exists no more and the terrors of memory have no place.

She turns to the back, pulls the cord around her neck. There is a moment of simulated strangling, and she does a back fall. She does not land in a position. She lands in a figureless sprawl, a blot on the ground, like one of those Rorschach blots. She lies there in nothingness.

But her memory of that mark of her death to her life, to her body and the world, will defile every other being who steps into that matter of her being, and passes through with boots forever stained with the memory of happiness. I know I see her rushing down a corridor, a columned corridor, frantic with this umbilical cord in her hands, frantic knowing she can have no peace from the demands of the crime except to die. And it is that rush that carries her to the great doors at the beginning, causes her to thrust them open into the room of her destiny, to close them and proceed to the bed. It is from that moment that I have taken the dance.

Once, when I was doing *Night Journey,* I had an awful cold and could not make it to a rehearsal. I tried, but I simply had no strength to leave my home. I was Jocasta and the ballet begins when I am about to kill myself with a rope, downstage, by the bed. It ends as it begins; it's a moment of flashback. I was at home, and another young woman was

As Jocasta in Night Journey, *May 3, 1947.*

dancing the role of Jocasta in rehearsal. I got a telephone call from an assistant at the theatre. "Martha, did you die by the bed in *Night Journey?*" In disbelief I answered, "Die upstage? Never!"

When I needed a bed for *Night Journey* I asked Isamu Noguchi to bring me a bed and he did, quite unlike any bed I had ever seen before. It is the representation of a man and a woman—nothing like a bed at all. He brought to me the image of a bed stripped to its bones, to its very spirit.

I met Isamu when I had a studio in Carnegie Hall, and his mother, who was Irish, was doing costumes for me. Isamu's father was Japanese and this wonderful combination of blood gave him a look that often made people mistake him for an Italian boy. He was young and vibrant with masses of curly hair. As he grew, he became more surely Japanese. That is the story of his life.

His sister, Ailes Gilmour, danced in my company. The first collaboration Isamu and I worked on was *Frontier,* in 1935, and we would continue to work together for the next fifty years. Our collaboration ended in December 1988, on the day that Isamu died; we were then still working on projects for the future. As was our way, we looked to the act of becoming, not to the past. Ours was purely, absolutely, a work relationship. I adored him, and I think he adored me. It never entered our minds to have anything except the best, and it never entered our minds to have a love affair. Never.

Isamu created his work mainly from some idea I gave him or some idea he gave me. I would perhaps give him the bones of an idea and he would return with something whole. I never told Isamu what to do or how to do it. He had a great feeling for space and its use on the stage.

A curious intimacy exists between artists in collaboration. A distant closeness. From the start, there was an unspoken language between Isamu and me. Our working together might have as its genesis a myth, a legend, a piece of poetry, but there always emerged for me from Isamu something of a strange beauty and an otherworldliness.

The designs that Isamu brought to *Frontier* came from our discussion of the hold the frontier had always had on me as an American, as a symbol of a journey into the unknown. Traveling to California by train, the endless tracks were to me a reiteration of that frontier.

When at last I asked Isamu for an image of them for my dance, he brought to me the tracks, as endless ropes into the future.

219

My mother was at the opening of *Frontier*. The people behind her said out loud that there must have been something wrong with one of my legs, because I had only used the left one in kicking. My mother turned around sharply and proudly and said, "I am her mother and she was formed perfectly at birth."

I remember the first time I did *Frontier* in Europe. A young woman came up to me after the performance and said, "Why do you call that dance *Frontier?* Frontier is the barrier of my own country. It's not anything big or expansive. When you reach the frontier, you've reached a barrier."

I had the idea of *Frontier* in my mind as a frontier of exploration, a frontier of discovery, and not one of limitation. I wonder what this young woman would say to me today, now that the Berlin Wall has been brought down. I saw it go up and now I have seen it come down. It makes me feel triumphant to think that nothing lasts but the spirit of man and the union of man. People cross the border from East to West to shake the hands of those they have not seen before. In a way, they have become each others' frontier.

When I needed a place for Medea onstage, the heart of her being, Isamu brought me a snake. And when I brooded on what I felt was the insolvable problem of representing Medea flying to return to her father the Sun, Isamu devised a dress for me worked from vibrating brilliant pieces of bronze wire that became my garment and moved with me across the stage as my chariot of flames.

For *Clytemnestra* I spent many evenings on the studio floor placing great pieces of red material around me. I had an idea, told it to Isamu, and he evolved a way to use fabric as both a costume and a prop—a triumphal cape as well as the entrance to Clytemnestra's bedchamber. I had used fabric in movement before, but not in an intense design way, such as this. I felt its necessity and so did Isamu. He was always very aware of what I needed to express.

Seraphic Dialogue was originally titled *The Triumph of St. Joan,* which premiered in 1951. This earlier work was presented as a solo. I danced all the aspects of Joan. I danced the Maid, the Warrior, and the Martyr. I left the stage to change my costumes while the orchestra played. One day while I was changing out of one costume into another, I suddenly felt that as a solo, the realization of the dance was not fulfilled. The story of St. Joan is very much a drama, and when I came to this conclusion, Isamu entered into it.

And then the dance became *Seraphic Dialogue.* I had no idea what Isamu would bring to me. I told him about my reading into the life of St. Joan, and my feelings about her. I had an idea; so had he.

When I went to his studio, I was dazzled by the beautiful set he had built. It is a very active piece, made of metal, a cathedral without limitations, like no other cathedral in the world. The doors opened. It was magic. When I realized that it could be unhinged, it opened up an entirely new area of movement for me. He called it his geometry of faith.

In *Legend of Judith,* my solo in which I retold the myth of the biblical heroine, the episode to represent "her putting aside her garments of sadness and putting on her garments of gladness" suggested to me a jewel to be worn and revealed on stage. But I was unprepared for the barbaric carved jewel necklace and headpiece that Isamu brought to me with which to

As Medea in Cave of the Heart *in the wire dress Isamu Noguchi designed for me,*
May 10, 1946.

dress myself within the dance. They intensified and gave me a deeper
image of myself as Judith, they in some way possessed the spirit of this
Jewish heroine. Downstage she puts on her garments: her necklace, her
belt, her fine lace, her great rings that go up her arm. This means to me,
"I am ready to do battle, I will do it, whatever I have to do." With Judith,
it was the gift of being a woman, an enticing female. She knew she was
in love with Holofernes, in a way. She antagonized him. She adored him.
But she never lost her purpose, which was that he must die. "In desire,"
she says, "I intend to kill you."

With my dear Isamu Noguchi.

The gesture of triumph I made toward the tent of Holofernes, which Isamu created as a rampant animal, came to me with added power in the coiled bracelet he had devised for my arm.

Often I would find that after Isamu and I had talked, he would bring me a maquette as a gift, perhaps so small it emerged from a matchbox. Shortly afterward, those delicate bits of magic would disappear, as did many of Isamu's maquettes: neither he nor I gave them away, so perhaps they will find their way home again. I hope they do. I miss them. Isamu knew me so well that if I began by saying, "Isamu, it is lovely but I need to think about it," he would snatch it from my hands and retreat, to return the next day with something completely new. But always Isamu brought to me his idea of space, the intimacy of an object onstage.

It was only with *Appalachian Spring* that I had a very definite idea for Isamu. I brought him to the Museum of Modern Art to show him Giacometti's construction *The Palace of Sleep at 4 A.M.* He was not very happy about going, but we went. And he understood immediately the quality of space I was looking for.

Isamu had sculpted a head of me. I did not like it then and I do not like it now. It had shown a side of my face, my left side, which changes only when I work. Isamu had seen this and caught it. He had seen too deeply this time, even for me.

For a time I was struggling to find the right stage setting for *Night Chant,* which has its roots in Indian lore. We needed a platform, an elevation from which the goddess, the priestess, would emerge. I was in the studio and across the room was the set Isamu had designed thirty years earlier, in 1958, for *Embattled Garden.* I turned it around to reveal its steps and its scars, all that was not seen before by the audience. I invited Isamu to a rehearsal and showed him how to use the old set in a new way, hoping that he would not refuse me the permission to do so. It was, in its way, an accident and this was a rather odd request. He was excited and pleased by the prospect. "Martha," he said, "all art is in some ways an accident, using accidents. Yes, of course, you may use the set in this way."

Several years ago, when I wanted to lure Isamu to create a work for my ballet *Frescoes,* I asked him to look at the rough outlines of that dance. He entered the studio, and I said, "Oh Isamu, I need your eyes."

He knew I was up to something because as we walked to our chairs he said to me, "Martha, make sure that is all you take." But I had already taken so much from Isamu, as had the world. It is said that the shamans, the holy men of the past, are the artists of today. For me it is in this path that Isamu walked and directed our blood memory. He took me to images that I had never contemplated before and gave new life to works I had created.

. . .

One of the two works Isamu made for me that touched me most deeply is the central image for *Hérodiade,* a dance that came as a great crisis in my life, in 1944. I had wanted the image of a woman, waiting and wandering within the landscape of her own psyche, her own bleached bones placed before the black mirror of her fate. When you look in the mirror, what do you see? Do you only see what you want to see and not what is there? If you are introspective you see your own death. A mirror is an instrument of introspection, its use is to search for the truth.

224

It is from the poem by Mallarmé that I took the image of a woman making herself up. She walks in, she walks toward the chair, she hesitates, moving backward from the chair; it is not time to begin. Then she sits on the chair and she possesses it by throwing her leg across it. The woman, the attendant, brings in the black mirror at the end and leaves it there. It is then that Herodias leaves her chair and, by doing so, out of the darkness enters the light again.

What Isamu brought to me was a haunting evocation. Deep within the bones was placed a small object, a bird. I sensed it was Herodias's heart, vibrating and exposed to life. "Skeleton," to me, is a flattering word. When I walk toward it, I walk into it. It was mine, too. And it still is. There is a particular walk that does it. We call it "the Dart." There is a constant focus on that one place where there is a living potential and the bird is there. There's a living potential for each one of us if we choose to take it. If we don't choose it, it is because we are afraid.

Whenever I danced *Hérodiade,* it was always to that animating force that I moved across the stage. It was for me the core of Isamu's heart as well, that part of each artist which, as he becomes as one with the sacrificial animal, he exposes to the world.

With composers, I have always wanted and demanded a collaboration. This is part of the rich legacy Louis Horst has given me, and I am grateful for it. There are only two choices: you either accept the composer's music or you do not. I think that it's important to state that the dance does not interpret the music; the music is a setting for the dance.

Hérodiade, *October 1944*.

When I work with a composer I usually give him a detailed script. In the script are notes I have taken from books I've been reading, quotes from this and that. There is a kind of order, a sequence I try to bring to the script in terms of placement and the means of the dancers. Here, for instance, I will note that there is to be a solo, and here a duet; this is to be the company, and this is to be a return to the solo, and so on, throughout the script. I never cut a composer's music. I never cut him down to time. When I get the music, I start to choreograph. I have never, ever, cut a note of music or even a rest of music, because if I do that, then what am I asking for? I do not want, nor do I need, a mirror of myself.

· · ·

Louis felt music very deeply. He made me aware of music, whether it was Aaron Copland or whether it was Scott Joplin. Louis felt that Aaron had a future in the dance and in the dance world and that he was willing and determined to use it.

The first music I used of Aaron Copland's was his Piano Variations in 1931, for the ballet I called *Dithyrambic*. It was, however, our collaboration years later for *Appalachian Spring* that remains most memorable. Most of the work I did with Aaron for *Appalachian Spring* was done through the mail. If the post office only knew what was transpiring between us. I was either in New York, Bennington, or Washington, and Aaron was elsewhere, mainly Mexico at the time. I accepted a commission from Elizabeth Sprague Coolidge to do three pieces for a Washington premiere at the Library of Congress; the other composers for the program were Darius Milhaud and Paul Hindemith. Right after Aaron accepted, Carlos Chávez accepted a commission to write a piece I later called *Dark Meadow*. I remember writing to Aaron, "I think I am the most fortunate dancer anywhere to have you and Chávez. I cannot believe it as yet."

It took a few scripts for me to get exactly what it was I wanted. Aaron thought the first one a bit too severe, and suggested, in his own way, a cross between the material I had given him and *Our Town*. It took me a bit of time to think this through. I wanted an American piece. In one of my original scripts I had envisioned the ballet with an episode from *Uncle Tom's Cabin*. There was also an episode with an Indian girl, specifically the thoughts of a pioneer woman when she sees an Indian girl on whose parents' land the frontiersmen have settled. She was to represent a dream, a figure always at the fence of our dream. It was the legend of Pocahontas, the legend of American land, youth, and country. It was a meeting of frontiersman and Indian. But it didn't work.

Neither did the Uncle Tom episode. Aaron felt the same way. Through a letter I wrote to him from Bennington I tried to define what I wanted:

Appalachian Spring *with Erick as the Husbandman and May O'Donnell as the* *Pioneer Woman, 1944.*

It is hard to do American things without either becoming pure folk or else approaching a little like a mural in a middle western railway station or post office.

You may object to some of the things, such as the use of the Indian girl. But please read it through and tell me if you think we can do it or if it defeats the end. I have thought of the use that Hart Crane made of her and also the "American Grain" of William Carlos Williams. I have as you will see taken out the *Uncle Tom's Cabin* episode altogether. I think you were right that it was dragged in by the hair of the head and I did not seem to be able to fix it so I started on a different aspect.

I have used the word "poem" several times in this. I know you will understand that I do not mean a tone poem but that I mean something nostalgic in the lyrical way and yet completely unsentimental and strong about our way. It has to do with the roots insofar as people can express them, without telling an actual story.

I do want to remember that it is for stage and that it will have certain incongruities that will make it at times delightfully theatrical if I can make it work.

Unfortunately, neither the episode with *Uncle Tom's Cabin* nor the Indian worked. Somehow the ideas of the dream of the Indian girl were conveyed in the ballet through other means. I sent off a revised script to Aaron who reacted favorably to the changes. I then wrote to him:

I was so relieved to get your letter with your re-action to the revised script this morning. I will say that mildly I have been on pins and needles. I am glad you think it is better than the first one. I do know that when I hear your music it will give a new and different life to the script. Once the music comes I never look at the script. It is only to make a working base for the composer and myself. Now it exists in words, in literary terms only, and it has to come alive in a more plastic medium, which music is to me. So please feel free to let the music take its own life and urge.

I am anxious to deal in movement rather than in words. It seems that I have written miles of words. I do know, too, that the ending will be better than I could devise as the music assumes its own life and character and that it will carry it through in a stronger way. Perhaps it is wrong to make you take that responsibility. But that is the way I work . . . to make a skeleton and then to be ready and willing to change when the music comes. The story is not so important, of course, as the inner life that emerges as the medium takes hold of the germ of the idea and proceeds to develop.

Reading in my bedroom at Bennington, with Henry Cowell's score of Deep Song *to the left.*

About a year later, in mid-June 1944, the music arrived, on a Friday afternoon as I was heading out the door for a weekend away. As soon as I returned home, I listened immediately to the music. "Thank you so much for a beautiful work," I then wrote to Aaron, "because I am sure the last of it is as beautiful as the first. It is a dream that I have had for so long, and now I can hardly realize that it is about to come true."

By August I was in Bennington preparing for the October premiere in Washington. I finally, after many weeks of delay, sat down and wrote to Aaron:

> I have been trying to write to you for weeks but I have been as occupied as you can imagine, and you can permit your imaginings to be quite extravagant. I have been working on your music. It is so beautiful and so wonderfully made. I have become obsessed by it. But I have been also doing a little cursing, too, as you probably did over that not-so-good script. But what you did from that has made me change in many places. Naturally, that will not do anything to the music. It is simply that the music made me change. It is so knit and of a completeness that it takes you in very strong hands and leads you into its own world. And there I am.
>
> The part I had not heard is really magnificent and the ending is wonderful. I also know that "The Gift to Be Simple" will stay with people and give them great joy. I hope I can do well with it, Aaron. I do not have any idea as to name yet so we must get together on that.

When Aaron first presented me with the music its title was "Ballet for Martha"—simple, and as direct as the Shaker theme that runs through it. I took some words from the poetry of Hart Crane and retitled it *Appalachian Spring*. When Aaron appeared in Washington for a rehearsal, before the October 30, 1944, premiere, he said to me, "Martha, what have you named the ballet?"

And when I told him he asked, "Does it have anything to do with the ballet?"

"No," I said, "I just like the title."

Appalachian Spring is essentially a dance of place. You choose a piece of land, part of the house goes up. You dedicate it. The questioning spirit is there and the sense of establishing roots.

The original score of *Appalachian Spring* was orchestrated for thirteen musicians. Aaron then decided to enlarge it. And so he made it an entity in itself. It now has an independent existence apart from the dance. It is a symbol for many people of the central part of America. They see distances which, perhaps, exist no longer.

I like to work from a piano score of the composer's music. He conceives it for an orchestra of however many instruments there are in his vision, then reduces it to a piano score from which I feel most comfortable working. At other times I will work in silence, blocking out movement before I find a piece of music, and then sometimes it works and other times it does not, and I have to discard things. For example, with *The Rite of Spring* I had known the music very deeply for years, but in preparation for my 1984 version I listened to the recorded music over and over again, so that by the time my first rehearsal came, I worked in silence to the music I now felt in my body as well as heard in my mind. I worked closely then with the pianist, asking him to guide me through the first reading of the music and subsequent readings, to notate the change of instruments for me.

I don't work from counts. I have a very physical memory. I work from body phrase.

A girl came up to me once after I had danced the bride in *Appalachian Spring*. She had an honest smile and said, "I know your dance is abstract."

I said, "Yes, abstract."

"Yet when you sit in the chair," she said, "you seem to be rocking a baby, and I know that can't be abstract."

I said, "That is exactly what it is. Every time you drink a glass of orange juice, you're drinking the abstraction of an orange. That's an abstraction to me: the whole effect."

My great-grandmother went from Virginia to Pennsylvania, her family in search of good soil to till. The Pioneering Woman in *Appalachian Spring* is modeled upon my great-grandmother as is the Ancestress in *Letter to the World*. She terrified me. She was very beautiful and was always very still. What her father did, and what was passed down in family lore, was wear his best Sunday shirt to do his farming in the belief in the nobility of physical labor, and before he did any work, she had to be sure to iron it each morning.

Each composer offers a new experience. In the spring of 1990, I went with my company to the Spoleto Festival in Charleston. Gian Carlo Menotti reminded me about our work together for *Errand into the Maze,* which was appearing on the program. I wrote for him a detailed script. He said I then went ahead and did a dance which had no relation to the script. At first he was very upset, but then he called Aaron Copland who said, "Oh Gian Carlo, she does that all the time."

That seemed to calm him down a bit. Gian Carlo also reminded me of a disagreement I had with Isamu when we were working with the stage props for the set of *Errand into the Maze*. Besides a very long rope to symbolize the maze, there was a piece stage right that resembled a curiosity but was actually designed by Isamu to be molded after a woman's pelvic bone. What better symbol for sexuality or the fear of it? But as beautiful as this set was, Isamu and I were not in agreement over something or other. This is the only time I can remember being angry with him. I had forgotten about it completely until Gian Carlo reminded me that I slapped Isamu across the face during the dress rehearsal. I chose not to remember this. I only hope that Isamu was able to forget it as well. I suspect I was going through my violent period.

Errand into the Maze, *February 28, 1947.*

. . .

Someone once asked me why I never created a dance based on the life of Marie Antoinette and I said I had no desire to dance European heroines. My interest was in America and the women of classical Greece. There was one, though, I think of now and that is Mary, Queen of Scots, in *Episodes,* where I choreographed the first half of the ballet and George Balanchine, the second. This was in May 1959, to the music of Anton Webern.

234

Lincoln Kirstein had invited Balanchine and me to lunch at the Pavillon restaurant. It was here that he presented the idea to us of joining our companies together to work with him in the theatre. Neither Balanchine nor I liked the idea very much. Lincoln, I think, was still trying to get back at me for standing up to him throughout the years. He suggested that Balanchine and I do a ballet together, hoping, I learned later, that my effort would fall flat on its feet. He suggested that I do something with a story line and that Balanchine do something abstract, both to the music of Webern.

I remember Balanchine came to my rehearsal to see the completed dance. I was surprised to see him without Lincoln. Balanchine seemed surprised at my question and said, "But Lincoln has nothing to do with artistic matters."

Lincoln started us off with a simple rule: I would dance first and no one would bow. I went first and danced the story of Mary, Queen of Scots. Walter Terry, a wonderful dance critic, had told me that Lincoln had confided to him that he felt my work would be old-fashioned compared to Balanchine, who was the avant-garde. It didn't quite work out that way. I brought down the house with applause, which must have been something of a disappointment to Lincoln. The audience would not stop to allow the performance to continue until my company and I had bowed. Lincoln was furious!

A few nights later I was speaking with Lincoln on the phone, now understanding a little better his reason for encouraging the collaboration. I asked him to repeat *Episodes* the following year, to which he replied, "*No*. Why should I?"

"Lincoln," I said, "if you do not repeat it, you are nothing better than a common thief."

We have not spoken since, which sorrows me. I loved Lincoln; he was a little odd at times, but who isn't?

Mr. Balanchine was so wonderful to work with, considerate and concerned—a joy to be with. It was equally exciting to work with Karinska, the Russian couturiere, who designed the costumes and spoke in a wonderfully pronounced English. I asked for a dress that would be like the dress I'd had Isamu Noguchi design for Medea in *Cave of the Heart*. My idea was to have a dress that Mary would wear onstage and then step out of so that she became a woman and the dress would stand onstage as a symbol of her as the queen.

Karinska took us to her room, which was filled with boxes overflowing with fabrics and feathers. All her acolytes surrounded her. She would say to one of them, "Bring me the box with the feathers. No, the other feathers. And the beading. Yes, the black beading."

Then when she was satisfied she turned to us and said, "Now you must leave, Kawinska, now she inwents."

I saw Antony Tudor as a dancer, as a choreographer, as a great figure in the dance world. I had been told he had worked with some of my former students and dancers. He came from England to work in the United States in the early 1940s. I was very much in awe of him. He was tall, slim, and distinguished in appearance. He began his career with the Ballet Rambert in 1930, dancing in some of Frederick Ashton's early works. As his dances developed he became more and more interested in the use of psychological elements in his dances.

He was what was known as a choreographer. Such an impressive word. I had never heard the word "choreographer" used to describe a maker of dances until I left Denishawn. There you didn't choreograph, you made up dances. Today I never say, "I'm choreographing." I simply say, "I am working."

I never cared much for choreographing. It is a wonderfully big word and can cover up a lot of things. I think I really only started to choreograph so that I could have something to show off in. It came as a great shock to me when I stopped dancing that I was honored for my choreography as well.

I loved the reaction of Samuel Goldwyn, whose words may have been mangled but were always inspired, when Garson Kanin recommended that I choreograph *The Goldwyn Follies*. Sam said, "I've heard of her. What kind of dance does she do?"

Garson brighted with "modern dance." To which Sam replied, "Not modern dance. It's so old-fashioned." He was right.

Modern dance dates so quickly. That is why I always use the term "contemporary dance"—it is of its time. I never, never say "modern dance." There is no such thing. The public may have called me modern, but I did not. And as for the avant-garde, Gian Carlo Menotti told me in Spoleto after my company had performed, "Everything in art changes, except the avant-garde."

Years after first meeting Antony Tudor I was talking backstage with him and he asked me how I would like to be remembered—as a dancer or as a choreographer. I said to Antony, "As a dancer."

He looked at me rather sadly and said, "I pity you."

When we got to know each other, Tudor came backstage to see me after a performance, and was less than pleased with what he had seen onstage. "At last," he said to me, "you have compromised."

And with that, I turned around and kicked him in the shin. He stayed until everyone had left to apologize and although I should have apologized as well, I didn't, but I loved and honored Antony.

Eighteen years ago, I was hospitalized for diverticulitis. When I returned home I received a telegram from Tudor which said, "I understand that once again you are revived, resuscitated, rejuvenated. Once again the phoenix. But Martha, I have always had a difficult time distinguishing between the phoenix and the harpy."

That was in the early 1970s when I had stopped dancing. I had lost my will to live. I stayed home alone, ate very little, and drank too much and brooded. Finally my system just gave in. I was in the hospital for a long time, much of it in a coma, all through it under the care of my beloved Dr. Allen Mead. It was felt I would not recover. The visitors trailed off after a while. I was not exactly delightful company, and the prognosis was depressing. A few friends remained, very few. And even they began to trail off. Ron Protas would come to sit with me. I told him later how much I had heard from the doctors when I wasn't supposed to, when I was in the coma.

Then, one morning, I felt something welling up within me. I knew that I would bloom again. That feeling, an errand into the maze, over and over in my mind, sustained me to go on. It was my only way to escape the constant fear of what might come.

Finally, the turning point came. By then, I was sitting up, out of the coma. I had for the only time in my life let my hair go white.

Agnes de Mille came to visit. She was a good friend through it all, and courageous soul that she is now, still stands with me, but at times, Agnes can say the absolute wrong thing, for the finest and most heartfelt reasons. This visit was no exception. "Oh Martha," she said with a smile, "I am so glad that you decided to let your hair go natural." When she left, I turned to the window and said to myself, "The hell I will." The next morning I had a colorist in, and somehow felt I would fight my way back. And I did, but it was more of a fight than I had anticipated.

The easiest part of recuperating was following the doctor's orders. Dancers are trained to be disciplined, to follow a regimen. To stop drinking was not a problem. I turned to it, perhaps more than I should have, when

Erick left me. My dependency increased when I began to feel my powers as a dancer leave me.

A dancer, more than any other human being, dies two deaths: the first, the physical when the powerfully trained body will no longer respond as you would wish. After all, I choreographed for myself. I never choreographed what I could not do. I changed steps in Medea and other ballets to accommodate the change. But I knew. And it haunted me. I only wanted to dance. Without dancing, I wished to die.

238

The last time I danced was in *Cortege of Eagles*. I was seventy-six years old. I had long been haunted by the image of Hecuba, the old and helpless Queen of Troy who watched as one by one, her loved ones died before her. I did not plan to stop dancing that night. It was a painful decision I knew I had to make.

When I stopped dancing, but kept making dances, it was very difficult at first to create not on my own body. Very, very difficult. I was not able to transfer it from myself. But now I know that I can, and I do. I thought of a good friend of mine, a painter, who could not paint after the death of her husband. "I can no longer paint," she told me. "What is there to paint?" Her canvas was bare and every day she stared at the whiteness, the blank canvas near a table of closed paints. And then one day she made, with a dab of paint, a mark on the canvas. And with that tiny spot, that brief conquering of available space, she began to paint.

When it is a dancer's time to leave, then he leaves. I never force anybody to stay. When a dancer wants to leave I say, "Go. It is your time. But the door is always open. You will always be welcome." And that has happened. It is happening now in my life. When it is time, it is time.

I recovered. But the path was not easy and was made more difficult because those I had placed in charge of my company did not want me back. They

Dancing the role of the Bride in Appalachian Spring
with Stuart Hodes, 1958.

were having a lovely time running things, though the company had all
but disappeared. Without my permission, the rights were given to allow
my company to appear on the same bill with two or three other dance
companies. When I was first presented with the idea, I absolutely forbade
it. Two of the dancers who did not want me back approached my friend
Arnold Weissberger and said, "This is proof Martha is forgetful. We told
her all about the shared performances last year, and she loved the idea.
And now, of course, she forgot. So sad. Poor Martha."

Arnold called me and laughed. "Martha," he said, "I knew they were
liars, but this last meeting confirmed it. They said you had forgotten the
shared programs. I told them, 'Impossible. One thing a star never forgets
is billing.' " And he was right.

Cortege of Eagles, *February 21, 1967.*

I returned from the hospital to my studio, and reorganized my company. I went on to choreograph ten new ballets and many revivals.

A few months before he died, Tudor came to my school to give a lecture. "Antony," I asked when he came through the door, "how has it been?"

"Terrible," he said.

"Sit down and tell me everything," I said.

That was the last time I saw Antony.

Many people ask me if it is difficult for a classical ballet dancer to learn my technique. The techniques are not so different. First they share a devotion to the dance as an excitement and as a power. They use that power whether in the ballet or in contemporary dance. My technique is basic. I have never called it the Martha Graham technique. Never. ⟦It is a way of doing things differently than anyone else. It is a certain use of the body. It is a freedom of the body and a love of the body. It is a love of the theatre as a vehicle through which a dancer can express himself.⟧

Many people have asked me why I did *Lucifer* with Rudolf Nureyev. Lucifer is the bringer of light. When he fell from grace he mocked God. He became half god, half man. As half man, he knew men's fears, anguish, and challenges. He became the god of light. Any artist is the bringer of light. That's why I did it with Nureyev. He's a god of light.

And Margot Fonteyn was such a glorious complement to him in it. Luminous as night. She was a bit wary of me at first, until a moment came when she had to dismount from a lift and it looked awkward. She and I both knew it, but nothing was said. I rechoreographed it so that several men covered her dismount. She knew what I had done and I knew she knew. She trusted me from then on. The only disagreement we had, if

Dancing in my late fifties: Cave of the Heart.

you can call it that, was over shoes. Margot wanted to be barefoot, and no matter how I explained that even I danced in slippers in *Appalachian Spring* and other ballets, she was adamant. How could she be a contemporary dancer in shoes? We are two very strong-willed Tauruses, Margot and I. It went on for days.

I was with my company in London, and after a performance of *Night Journey,* Nureyev came backstage to meet me. He had recently defected, in 1963. Maude and Nigel Gosling brought him soon after he left Russia to see my performance as Jocasta. When we met afterward, he simply stared and said nothing. I wondered if he did not like my dance, or perhaps couldn't speak English. I only found out years later, after he and I became friends, when he told me he was so moved he felt speechless. Later when I was no longer dancing Jocasta, he told me he'd finally gotten around to noticing the other choreography. Rudolf is Russian, but I began to realize he had an Irish tongue.

I have had former members of the Kirov in my company—Rudolf Nureyev and Mikhail Baryshnikov. It makes me smile to think that years ago my company and I were denied visas to the Soviet Union, because I was what they called a bad influence on the young. I took it as a supreme compliment. And now, of course, they want me more than ever. They themselves have changed. They are no longer back in the sixties or seventies. They want to be of this age.

A few years ago, at a gala in New York, Maya Plisetskaya, prima ballerina assoluta of the Bolshoi Ballet, danced Michel Fokine's *The Dying Swan.* Some people were surprised to see such a classic dancer in so classic a piece on a program with *Letter to the World* and *El Penitente*. But all dance is universal, and there are only two kinds of dance, good and bad.

I want the dancers in my company not to be like me. I want them to have studied with me, of course. I want them to be themselves and I encourage them to do that. I want the dancers to learn the dance physically, strongly, and then put their own meaning into it, if they can dare to do that. I don't believe in having stereotyped mes running around. What a horrible thought. They should bear the marks of my work while feeling free to be the individuals they are.

I felt that always with Baryshnikov, Nureyev, and Fonteyn. I was scared to death of them at first. I thought they were the absolute epitome of the ballet world as it was then. They never crossed me. They were easy to work with. They did what I could find for them to do that was different from what they had done before. They relished that. They had a supreme appetite for life, for the people in it.

What I had to do with each of them was, of course, to teach them the dance. They didn't learn by counts. No real dancer I know learns counts. They phrase, and each dancer has to learn that and then accommodate it to his body. And that's exactly what we did.

They were all very responsive, warm, and very exciting in their ability to do a new thing. They constantly did new things for me and for themselves. It was an entirely new experience for all of us. When it came time to revive Miss Ruth's *The Incense* I thought Maya Plisetskaya was the only one who with her extraordinary arms and presence could convey this mystical solo of Miss Ruth's, who as a temple dancer with the simplest of gestures placed incense into the burners, and taking the smoke into her body became the smoke. Maya loved the film I showed her of Miss Ruth dancing, but she had a tour in Spain at that time. It couldn't be changed. She was saddened. We embraced. She left the studio and suddenly, a minute later, the doors flew open and Maya walked a few steps toward me, did Miss Ruth's arm ripples perfectly, said not a word and exited. I turned to Ron and said, "She'll do it." And she did.

When I first saw Margot Fonteyn she was a great and beautiful figure. The magic of Margot's presence is an elusiveness of spirit that defies description. Margot was intrinsically herself, innocent and open onstage. She reminds me of that line from Chaucer: "I am my owne woman wele at ease."

No one could be a more severe critic of Margot than Margot. I remember watching her during a performance of *La Bayadère* while I stood in the wings. She had done the performance, had received thunderous applause and ovations, yet when the curtain came down for good she threw herself on the floor in tears because she felt that she had danced it so badly. She had not met her own standard, no matter how loud the praise. She was very young in spirit. Only Nureyev, her partner, could take her from hysteria. He whispered something to her and she began to laugh that wonderful laugh that is only Margot's, a reluctant laugh. Later, Rudolf told me he whispered every shocking obscenity he could think of. I believed him. The Goslings said that when he left Russia the first English he wanted to learn was the naughty words.

The only real problem with Rudolf was early in our *Lucifer* rehearsals. He kept coming later and later to rehearsal. Finally when he ambled in a full thirty minutes late, I looked up and said, "I think I am going to be angry. I am angry." With that, the dancers scattered. I went up to Rudolf and let him have it. I don't know if I would have had I known his reputation for talking back. But then again, I probably would have, with my black Irish temper. I told him he was a great artist but a spoiled, willful child. And that was just for starters. He only stammered and apologized. It must have done some good. He was never late again.

One of the most magnificent statements of Rudolf Nureyev as an artist was made the season he performed without a fee to help us, as did many others, including Misha and Margot. While Rudolf knew that he might never perform the title role in *El Penitente* for years, if ever, as he was rushing to make a plane to Paris, without time to take off his makeup, he dashed up to me and asked, "What are my corrections?"

Like Misha and Rudolf, Margot broke the rules and made her own path. She even broke a rule of geography, for wherever she danced, she was the center of the stage; wherever she stood, she held that silence and stillness . . . and our hearts.

Misha and Rudolf danced together in *Appalachian Spring,* Misha as the Husbandman and Rudolf as the Preacher. People ask me why I chose this dance for them; frankly, I did it because I believe it is a good theatre piece, and I present it as that.

One incident I shall never forget is when Margot, Rudolf, and I agreed to do the Blackglama mink ad, "What becomes a legend most?"—a difficult undertaking, at best. To begin with, the young man in charge of the campaign had the inspired idea that he would only give two coats, though there were three of us. Polly Bergen, a board member and friend, in very sweet tones, convinced him otherwise. Then Margot decided we should have six extra skins, "for a hood or something," and if they asked why, "it is because we are Martha, Margot, and Rudolf." On the day of the shooting, the man in charge, though he had been warned not to make any great preparations of food, went ahead and did it anyway. Rudolf, Margot, and I entered, and when in a Southern accent he said, "Mr. Nureyev, I have prepared some food for you," Rudolf, who took an instant dislike to him, snarled, "I do not know you. I will not eat your food."

The actual moment of the photograph, however, was great fun and I cried out, "This is when we throw the baby to the wolves," a reference to the Russian fable of a family fleeing across the ice and having to sacrifice one child to save the rest.

The man in charge thought I was just wonderful, a legend and so on, until we ran into a disagreement. He wanted to reprint the photograph in

Posing with Rudolf Nureyev and Dame Margot Fonteyn.

a book, but Rudolf refused outright. When I was asked if I would allow my portion of the photograph to be used alone, I said, "I will do nothing to go against Rudolf." Suddenly, to the young man, I became "an arthritic old hag" when he referred to me in conversation with others. It seems he wanted an invitation to the White House when I was to receive the Medal of Freedom from President Ford. When at first it couldn't be done he said, "I don't care, but the mink breeders will be angry." When my friend Diana Vreeland heard this she said, "Angry mink breeders, oh Southern airs and fine graces." I hadn't heard that phrase for a long time.

Misha came into my life, as a divine gift from God. Our lives converged; he defected and came to the United States and later danced with my company. His was the most perfect Husbandman in *Appalachian Spring* I had ever seen. I can never forget the section Misha was having trouble with, a run to his bride. Misha looked over to me for motivation. He brightened when I said, "Misha, you haven't seen her for five minutes." And his Penitent was even stronger than Erick's, who originated it. What I would have given to have danced with him, or with Rudolf.

While Misha was head of the American Ballet Theatre, we agreed that his company would be granted the right to perform certain of my ballets. In principle, I'm not against having my ballets done by other companies. The problem is *how* they are done. We are a small company with a large deficit. We cannot afford to spend the time to teach other companies our dances; we would have no time to organize our own fundraisers.

247

Diana Vreeland and I at a party after a performance.

Rehearsing American Document *with Misha, 1989.*

Misha agreed that our dances would be monitored, and would be coached properly. But this by no means suggests that we are going to go into a wholesale attempt to let every other company do my ballets. In the past, other companies have approached me wanting to have this ballet or that one. They want it and of course they want to be able to perform it within two weeks. That, of course, is absolutely impossible!

Misha also journeyed to Washington to speak for me before a congressional committee to get funding for the filming and preservation of my works. The money would not have come from the Arts Endowment, nor hindered it. It was lobbied against by the Endowment and much of the arts community is the loser. That tears my heart.

· · ·

I give the dancers a technique. Technique is a language that makes strain impossible. Then they do what they will with it. Sometimes the technique is taught badly, and I am very upset with it. In Cairo after we'd had several performances with a local company, a sign was put up after I left: "MARTHA GRAHAM TECHNIQUE TAUGHT HERE." They'd never seen dance in this aspect. It did not mean for them what it means for me—technique as a science. An absolute science. I can tell you what the shoulder means. I can tell you what comes from ballet. I can tell you where the arm comes from in the back and all of the excitement of where in the body it grows. I don't know how many years it took to learn certain things. But I enjoyed it. I enjoyed the physical engagement with myself.

249

Honored at the Kennedy Center with Ella Fitzgerald, Tennessee Williams, Aaron Copland, Rosalynn Carter, and Henry Fonda.

Teaching the role of the Chosen One in The Rite of Spring *to Terese Capucilli, as rehearsal director Bert Terborgh looks on, 1985.*

There is one bit of technique, which takes sixteen beats, that I have always used to instruct students. Imagine that the crown of your head is on your feet and you must bring the rest of your head down to join it. Let the soles of your feet come together like a prayer. There is a high lift on the counts of two and four, with the entire body in a seated position rising from the floor. The movement is coming up from the base of your body to the top of your head.

For the deep release, there is a deep breathing in of air, and then expelling it out in a deep contraction. For the contraction I see the heavens; for the deepening over I see the earth. For the release I view the earth over a cliff. For the high lift, I dwell within. There are also deep contractions, forward and backward. It is almost a rocking movement to the front and back, an unwinding. You are a diviner and you cast your sticks and get no answer. You cast them again, but still no answer. You try again until finally you lift your body up, open your arms and, yes, you finally have it.

For the contraction to the floor with a high arch: When arching back, think of Joan of Arc resisting a sword that is piercing her chest.

For the contraction, the expelling of the air in your body from the pelvis upward: Every study involves continuity. Pull, pull on the contraction. Do not cave in. And the contraction is not a position. It is a movement into something. It is like a pebble thrown into the water, which makes rippling circles when it hits the water. The contraction moves.

For the half pleadings: It is a position with the body on the floor, a slight contraction in the body, with the breath in, the arms at the sides cupped open to the sky.

For the use of the head and body: Think of Michelangelo's *Pietà*, or that extraordinary Bernini *Ecstasy of St. Theresa*. I have seen a photograph of a rock singer with that same look of exaltation.

For demi-pliés: Think that there are diamonds on your collarbone catching the light.

For the carriage of the arms, which is the most difficult for any dancer: Think of the arm as an extension of the spine. The upper arm is connected with love as in hugging. The use of the upper arm is apparent in all the best dancers.

When you have to do the same movement over and over, do not get bored with yourself, just think of yourself as dancing toward your death. In *The Rite of Spring,* when I danced the Chosen One, as I did so many continuous times, and came to my moment of finality, I thought of my rebirth.

For the knee vibrations, that bit of technique where from a standing position you are required to throw your leg up and swing it to your chest, and back behind your body and forward again: I always tell the student to think of the three witches in *Macbeth,* stirring the caldron endlessly, but with a purpose: "Double, double, toil and trouble. Fire burn and caldron bubble."

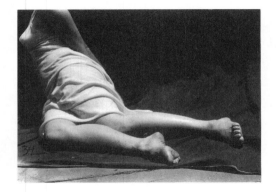

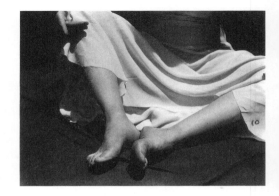

Imogen Cunningham movement series, Santa Barbara, California, 1931.

Horses have always given me wonderful images for teaching. In *Night Journey,* when I danced Jocasta, there is a difficult moment when you contract and your leg flies up. I always give the students the image of a horse rearing up. For my company member who portrays Jocasta, God help her, I say the movement represents the bite of remembrance rising up and fleeing through your mouth.

For our prances, a movement with much joy and gaiety, I am fond of telling my dancers it's like a lovely horse. You see this beautiful creature, and he is so charged with life, like the Lippizaner horses in Vienna. They love what they do. They are just dying to perform onstage, just as a dancer should be.

Agnes de Mille would audition large groups of people, and would always make the first elimination by watching their walk. It tells everything. I tell my students to walk across the room as if their hearts are on the wall. If this does not enliven them I add, "Remember, one day you will all die." That usually does it.

My dancers never fall to simply fall. They fall to rise. When Margot Fonteyn first saw us perform, she noticed how different our falls were from those of the Royal Ballet: "Why, we fall like paper bags. You fall like silk."

A dancer's art is built on an attitude of listening, with his whole being. When I speak of the need of listening to your own body, I never fail to talk about that wonderful lion at the beginning of MGM films. When he turns to the side, he turns so completely. He goes back and listens to his lioness, listens to his own inner being. He has that ability to draw back instead of waiting for somebody to look at him. He listens. To what? To himself. And the body is held back to the point where it can move.

Dancers' faces are curious. Dancers have more bones than most people and on the days when you work hard you are sure that you have somehow accumulated more bones than you started with. Dancers' faces are full of bones. I looked at Alicia Markova. There is that face, the bones. I looked

A joyous moment with my dancers.

at Nora Kaye. Same bones. I looked at some of the men. Same bones. Why? Because the constancy of the exercise makes your flesh lie back against your frame.

Onstage, timing is everything, and the subtleties are very difficult to teach. You must know how to hold the audience and when to drop the impact you have created. Miss Ruth was a master of this.

The bow is part of that impact and important to the performance. Years ago, when I lectured at the New School for Social Research in Manhattan, I stated that Pavlova bowed beautifully. I was much criticized for it, especially by ballet choreographer Michel Fokine, who was in the audience.

In the early days, before bows, we did run-ons. Mine was very quick. I would run to center stage, whip my body around to bow with urgency. In that same thrust of movement I would turn and run off. I had to be quick in case the applause did not last.

Many people have asked me if I have a favorite role, or if I am identified with a particular role. To which I always an-

255

swer that my favorite role is the one I am dancing now. You don't build on security. You risk. Everything is a risk. You use every part of anything you remember as part of the present, the now.

There are always people coming asking for autographs. The oddest one was after a college performance. It was a cold, late evening. I was just stepping into the car to go home when a young man came running breathless into the car headlights.

I had no paper or pen, and neither did he.

"I'm sorry," I said, "but there's nothing here to write with."

He threw himself on the front of the car and said, "Oh, you don't have to give me your autograph. Here is my program. Just spit on it."

Once, during a performance I attended at the Metropolitan Opera House, a sincere-looking young man came up to me and asked for my autograph, then shortly afterward, a woman who took a piece of paper from her shoulder bag. I was sitting in the balcony—not much money, you know—and I signed her paper. I was about to hand it back to her when she said, "Thank you, but who are you?"

I took the piece of paper, dropped it over the edge and as it fluttered down I said, "Find out."

Just before I turned *Frontier* over to another dancer, a very fine photographer, Barbara Morgan, came to see me and said, "Martha, I think it is a disgrace that you changed *Frontier*."

I said, "Changed it? It is not changed at all."

She said, "Then why did you change the dress?"

I said, "But I did not change a thing!"

"You most certainly did," was her reply.

And I said, "Darling, I made the dress. I had to sew it myself and there was only that one dress ever made and it was mine."

She still did not believe me. In other words, people sometimes see

what they imagine, not what really happens, nine times out of ten. And when Barbara came backstage to me after a performance of *Deaths and Entrances,* we disagreed once again.

"I'm sorry, Martha, that you didn't bring that man onstage again during the final entrance."

"What man?" I asked, while I sat at my dressing table and removed my makeup. I could see Barbara's reflection in the glass behind me.

"Merce Cunningham," she said.

And I said, "Well, he never did come in on the entrance."

"He most certainly did," she said.

"I should know," I said. "Maybe he should have come on in the choreography, but I never brought him on."

I have a photo Philippe Halsman took of me in which I am doing a backfall, lit by a strobe light. This movement I used in *Deaths and Entrances.* The title for the ballet is from a poem of Dylan Thomas's. The dance is about the lives of the three Brontë sisters, and in it many people try to see the autobiography of my sisters and me. One woman came backstage after the premiere and said, "How unrealistic to fall backward in a black evening gown. I never would do it."

I answered, "Neither would I. But haven't you ever been in a room where someone you loved, who no longer loved you, walked in, and your heart fell to the floor?"

At that moment she seemed to understand the communication of movement she had seen on the stage. She felt something, and that is all that I can ask from a member of the audience.

I think one has a right to his own personal life and I believe in a very full life. I don't believe in a convent life or an isolated life and I don't go into the lives of the company at all. They have their own lives. We are on a working basis and we respect one another. But I have no right to influence them in any way. I might think something is a little foolish, but it's not my business. I'm not a missionary, you see.

I have always encouraged members of my company to do their own dances. I have had little workshops, and within my company I have had Paul Taylor, Merce Cunningham, and many more perform their own works onstage. I don't arbitrarily select anyone; it just evolves. I may say that this person has the quality of a great dancer, but I cannot predict the future. He is either good or he is going to be not very good. Very often I will see someone in class who has great potential and I will try to develop that person. I have two or three now that are like this. They have to be completely technically wise. They must have a sense of how wonderful technique is—the wonderful quality that can be brought out through the technique.

259

I have asked Jerome Robbins to create a dance for my company. And to my joy, he has agreed. Jerry and I met years ago. We were walking together and ended up at Brentano's bookshop. It was winter and we went inside to warm up and look at the books. Jerry was in a creative doldrum even deeper than mine. I decided to buy him a book to cheer him up, *Macbeth*. It seemed to help.

Soon after, during World War II, we were both selected by Roseland to receive their dance award, "Tops in Terpsichore." Jerry called me to be his date and I agreed. I was more than a little nervous. I should have done more than hesitate. I should have run. The smoky dance hall was filled with jitterbugging sailors who couldn't have cared less about our awards. When the emcee stopped the music for the presentation, the crowd grew angry and restless. I was introduced as "appearing nightly on Broadway," and Jerry, as a young new choreographer. When we were presented

Clytemnestra *with Paul Taylor, 1958.*

with our awards we were horrified that the inscriptions were misspelled and read "Tops in Terpisscore." We took off immediately—not even onstage did I time a quicker exit.

Everyone wants to know about inspiration. Even Agnes sat with me years ago and suddenly blurted out, "Martha, how did you do it?" I wish I knew. Things wouldn't be so awful to contemplate if I knew. You never really know, you just sense those dreadful, inevitable footsteps following that make you go forward and work. I don't think in art there is ever a precedent; each moment is a new one and terrifying and threatening and bursting with hope. Often I am asked what I think will be the future of dance. I always answer if I knew I would want to do it first. But you never really know.

My only passion is to work, to be what St. John Perse calls born to the instant, the now. To become part of that one constant in life, our only constant—change.

It has been my great joy to work with so many talented friends. But it is more than a little scary. Liza Minnelli reminded me that when we were to start work on the ballet I did for her, *The Owl and the Pussycat*, in 1978, I took her hand and said, "You know, you are a terrible responsibility."

Darling Liza, how generous she has been to me. When I fell ill years ago, she was one of the first, she and our board chairman, Evelyn Sharp, to call and offer to help pay for the nurses. Every artist gets down to practicalities. We have no choice.

When Liza worked with the company, she was sensitive to everyone. She seemed like just another young girl, part of the scene. When the dancer who stood in for her in *Owl* looked a little sad, knowing Liza would be dancing the opening, Liza would invariably move to her with a sweet word. She is a very loving person. When I needed her to perform with us in Covent Garden, she brought her whole staff, paid for everything just to stand by me. I shall never forget the first day of rehearsal in London. We left the stage door and scads of young girls ran after Liza for her autograph. None of them came to me. Why should they? How could they know who I was? But suddenly out of nowhere they were fighting for my autograph. I found out later that Liza had noticed I was being ignored and quickly told the young girls they were basically idiots, that they were missing my autograph and I was just as much a legend as her mother, Judy Garland. That did the trick . . . but only Liza would have been so painfully sensitive to another's situation.

·   ·   ·

Then there was my collaboration with the actress Kathleen Turner. She had for years been a financial supporter of the company and when I asked if she would play the Speaker in *Letter to the World* she kindly agreed. Nowhere has the expression "Movement never lies" been truer than when I watched Kathleen at that first rehearsal. She was generous, sweet, and caring, but her body cried out, "Oh, my God. What have I gotten myself into?" I tried to change things to make it a more comfortable role for her, but I think I only made it worse, and so I let her find her own path, her own way, and she did.

262

Madonna came as a young student to my school. At first, she would come two hours early to watch me come in. She came to visit me after she had become famous. Everyone was terrified of my reaction. They couldn't have been more mistaken. I liked her tremendously. She is forthright. She is going to get what she wants and to hell with you. She is a maverick. Yes, she is criticized. She is naughty and dares you to react. But she only puts onstage what most women hide and yes, it may not be respectable.

In 1980, a well-meaning fundraiser came to see me and said, "Miss Graham, the most powerful thing you have going for you to raise money is your respectability." I wanted to spit. Respectable! Show me any artist who wants to be respectable.

Long before all of this I was given my first company performance in London. My friend Robert Helpmann, the former leading male dancer of the Royal Ballet, was appearing across the alley in another theatre in George Bernard Shaw's *The Millionairess,* with Katharine Hepburn. Their curtain was much earlier than mine so often Kate and Bobby would stand in the wings and watch me dance in my last ballet. Years later, a critic wrote he saw signs of my technique in her brilliant last soliloquy in the

Backstage with Madonna after the world premiere of Maple Leaf Rag, *October 1990.*

film *Long Day's Journey into Night.* I didn't see it at all. Kate is so uniquely herself. I don't think she ever needed an outside inspiration, ever.

Some years ago at a school in Georgetown, in Washington, a fourth-grade class studied my life as part of their syllabus. They watched the films that we have managed to make; they came to local performances, and from these sent me mail—letters and drawings—of what all this meant to them. One letter said, "I'd like to see *Lamentation* as a dance of joy." Another boy wrote that he felt *Lamentation* was too short, but when he thought this over, he decided that one could not stay sorrowful for too long and it was right that the dance was short.

Outside Covent Garden with Linda Hodes and a beautiful sheepdog.

When these children went to the theatre, they knew the color of the costumes, the designs of the sets, how the hair was arranged, who danced what and when. And I can tell you one thing for certain: they know who dances well and who does not. To me, this is real education and the children are left with a lasting mark.

Today, there are children's classes at my school. I love working with children. I would shake hands with them and call them by their first names.

As part of a gala a few years ago with American Ballet Theatre, the youngest children performed onstage. They each recited their names, and said together, "I love the earth. I love the sky. I love the world around me."

I wanted them to be named, not to remain anonymous people. They looked at the sky, they lifted their arms out. "My name is . . ." Nobody else has that name. Each one is a potential star and it is this ability to see themselves as unique that we hope to accomplish in class. They're special and I want them to be regarded as such.

One day a new girl came into the class. She was very full of herself and misbehaved wildly. One of the older dancers went to this girl and said, "We don't behave like that in this school." She stopped it. She was judged by her peers, and when you're seven or eight years old, it has an effect.

I remember telling one five-year-old who was watching a rehearsal that he could, in a few years, study with the eight- to ten-year-olds. He did not look very interested until I told him that we served milk and cookies after class.

Children learn the first part of a dancer's world—if you have to leave the floor you should never exit through the center while the others are dancing. You walk around the edge—you never, never interfere. If you come in late you never go to the middle of the floor; it is not nice. Besides, you can bring in bad things from the street to the floor.

I try to give children the excitement of dance. I explain to them what they are doing, how they are breathing. You can be Eastern or Burmese or what have you, but the function of the body and the awareness of the body results in dance and you become a dancer, not just a human being.

No matter the age of the student, the message I want to convey through the teaching of movement is the same. I want my students, above all, to be in rhythm and time, not just participating in something that has no relationship to the other dancers or to the music. What I look for in a teacher is the ability to find those little bits and pieces of the students—

Exchanging gifts with Mrs. Bush at the White House.

to go over and touch them where they are wrong. They are being taught and should have individual attention. Touching is very important. Through touch you can tell exactly where motivation comes from in the body. It is a tension and it is a release. I touch to show the thigh muscles, or the use of the back in motion. How a dancer turns in, how he does not.

If I had to present one ballet to a child of six or eight—and choosing one is no easy task—I would choose *Errand into the Maze*. This dance exemplifies, through the use of the rope on the floor and the object in the air, the strange place you are venturing into, something a child might understand. It is a conquering of fear—to find that one place onstage where the bird that makes you want to dance lives.

When I danced *Errand* at Radcliffe once, a young woman came up to me after the performance and said, "I love that dance. I go through that here every morning."

That I cannot vouch for, but I do know that during our State Department tour, while in Iran, we had to take a very small airplane, a DC-3 from Abedon to Teheran, with a cruising altitude of five thousand feet. We were traveling through snowstorms, like the paperweights of our childhood, alongside snow-capped mountains. The plane did everything but fall down. We had to turn back. I sat there and did *Errand* three times in my mind before we landed. It meant to me the passage through the unknown into life. And we did arrive safely in Teheran.

I have said to many children, "Do what you are doing and be excited about what you are doing. Be the best in your world by what you do and love it." I always say have a great love for what you are doing. Go to great lengths, good and bad, to do your absolute best. The audience will understand that. The audience is your judge and your only reality. I am not a romantic. I believe you must have a demonic technique and as Louis said, "Go at your audience at times with a whip." In those early days a favorite of mine, the critic Stark Young, said to a friend, "Must I join you at Martha's dance concert tonight? All that percussive angular movement— I am so afraid she'll give birth to a cube."

I want all of my students and all of my dancers to be aware of the poignancy of life at that moment. I would like to feel that I had, in some way, given them the gift of themselves.

·   ·   ·

Halston, the great clothes designer of the sixties and seventies, knew about the appetite for life. It is hard for me to talk about my dear friend, whose loss I feel every day. I think that I saw the best in him, which spoke to the best in me. I do feel the privilege of having known and worked with such a generous being. We had worked together, been collaborators, for at least fifteen years. Our first meeting was by chance.

I was to present the Capezio Dance Award to Robert Irving and there was nothing in my wardrobe I could wear, and nothing I could afford to buy. Then I thought, Leo Lerman, darling Leo, he knows the world. I called him, and Leo came back with the answer: Halston said he never lent things like that but for Martha Graham he would be honored. We drove up Madison Avenue to his building.

Halston suggested a wonderful earth-colored cashmere caftan and a darker natural poncho over it. I loved it. It felt as if I had always worn it. Halston understood the drape of fabric, and the body's movement beneath it; he understood elegance.

We then drove to David Webb's, and he lent me the most magical ruby and emerald string of beads. I went to the ceremony. The next morning reality dawned. But I just couldn't part with my Halston. I asked Halston if I could pay it off monthly. He said, "Martha, if I cannot give you that dress, there is nothing in the world I can give you."

From that point on we became friends. We would discuss costumes and ideas, and I told him how I used to shop for fabrics on Fourteenth Street and Orchard Street. By this time my hands were so crippled by arthritis that I always wore gloves. I could no longer search out fabrics and, most importantly, my hands had lost the ability to craft. It was and still remains a very painful thing.

We were in his workroom looking at new fabrics, running the skeins through our hands. I could not feel the material because of the gloves.

"I cannot use my hands," I told him, looking down at the long black gloves that covered my bent hands.

Celebrating with Liza Minnelli and Halston.

"Martha," he said, "let me be your hands."

And that is how our collaboration began. He would say, "I like that woman's body. I like that man's body. I see them in a glorified way, and I'd like to do something for them."

When one of my dancers goes onstage in a Halston costume, it is beautifully made, inside and out, and adds to the integrity of the movement. It must reveal the body, reveal the beautiful line of the waist, the hips, the shoulders, the turn of the head. The costume must speak to all of these things.

Halston was a strange, gentle, and fierce man. Fierce because he would only settle for the best. If you couldn't give your best, then too bad for you. He made that very clear in the beginning. Halston believed as did I that the only sin was mediocrity.

Halston, at one of the lowest ebbs in my life, came to me, helped my company to go on, and gave me a new image of myself to fulfill. And in that way he changed my life, just as he changed the face of American fashion through his gifts. Without him, my company would not exist today.

I cannot fully believe that he is gone. Halston came to see me just before he left for his new home in San Francisco. He came to tea and we talked and dreamed and planned and joked, just as we did each New Year's Eve we would spend together. He had a superstition that you had to work and to make plans for the New Year that evening, so that you would have a success, and he was right. But more important than success, you had less fear, you were attempting to plan your year, your destiny. The visit for tea was so poignant for me, haunted by the unspoken thought between us, that we would never see each other again.

Napoleon, when he had to decide to hire a mercenary general, would listen to all his credentials, and then ask, "But is he lucky?" And I know that I have been lucky. All the necessity in the world, all the drive, all the desire cannot help without it. How else could I have come back just three years ago from an illness from which it was felt I would not recover? I could not even speak or swallow. It was a small blood clot they told me later, a stroke, but it was enough to incapacitate me. Ron would come, so would Linda, Chris, Michele, Jayne, Richard, Peggy and Diane, and later wonderful nurses, Anne, Kitty, Helen, Maureen, to help me through and into the light. And Ron would read my favorite books to me, and talk and talk. He was like the Martha my grandmother described as having a tongue hung in the middle. But I didn't mind. I needed talk then. I didn't even care if he kept prowling around my room at times in his nervousness. It would have been terrible to be alone at this time. For in the back of my mind, I could still hear the young doctor saying, "At ninety-four, people just don't come back."

The blow struck so quickly, from nowhere. One moment I was preparing to have a guest to tea, another unable to speak, but understanding everything. And just managing to tell Ron and my nurses I was so sorry. I repeated *Errand into the Maze* over and over again in my mind. Those were lifelines to go on.

Perhaps one of the hardest tasks in my struggle to get back was to persuade Dr. Mead to let me out a little early. They had said I would need weeks to recover. I tried to explain that I had an entire company waiting for me to begin a new work in just seven days. It would be the best medicine. Oh, I tried everything. I must have driven them crazy because I did leave early.

Each day I came in to rehearse for just a little while. Slowly I was able to stay at least two hours in the afternoon and evening. Ron and Linda translated to the dancers when I grew weary and my voice was not clear. And I came back; I found my voice again. A therapist came once to see me. I listened to her with absolute attention and went through all of her exercises. Then I said to her gently, "I want to show you something." And with that I held my feet out straight before me. I was seated. I did some pliés and other stretching exercises in silence. I am sure she must have thought I had lost my mind. Then I said, "You see this means something to me. I can understand it. It is relevant to my life, to my body. What you have shown, as wonderful as it is, means nothing to me. It is not my way. I must find my own way." And I did.

Eight months later I finished my ballet *Night Chant*—the title taken from a Navaho ritual, the Yabechi, a healing ceremony—with its Navaho flute music and images of the Southwest. *Night Chant* received some of my best reviews.

Halston was now very ill in San Francisco. Something in my voice must have told him when we spoke by telephone, which we did every day, that

At a gala fundraiser with Associate Director Ron Protas.

I needed a holiday. He made it possible, called our business manager, Michele, and everything was done to the last detail. A vacation to the Southwest. He knew that I needed a vacation and he supplied the means for me to have it. He knew what this area of the country meant to me— its barrenness and its strength, its sky and its landscape.

I arrived in Tucson in June 1989. It was, for me, a sad time. My sister Geordie, whom I had visited for the last ten years since she had moved here from New York, had died a few months before, my last link to my parents and to my early life. If it had not been for Rachael and Gertrude, the nurses who looked after her, her time would have been much shorter. I planned to see them before I went back to rehearsal in New York with my company. As I looked up to the sky, I saw a Kiowa Rain Shawl, a beautiful cloud formation. And in front of me, the great saguaro cactus.

Its curious prehistoric shape has a power that hits me hard. You cannot help but feel some part of its magic come into your being, just as I have said that strange gestures come to all dancers, perhaps to all of us, if we will accept them.

The plan had been to come to Tucson to look at a Catholic girl's school that Mark Bahti, a trustee and friend who lived in Arizona, had found as a possible second home for our dance company. But first I wanted to visit Mark's fantastic shop of American Indian works of art. It had been his father Tom's life work. Tom had been a great friend to the Indians. They always brought him their very best things. But one of Tom's greatest treasures was not American Indian. He had a handwritten note from Georgia O'Keeffe. It hangs in the shop now, with a salutation only Georgia could summon up and execute in that forthright hand of hers: "Greetings Tom Bahti!"

As we drove up the roadway, the building we were to consider looked a little forbidding, very Gothic—not exactly my favorite period. It had been for over sixty years the home of the Sisters of the Immaculate Heart. At a press conference, when a reporter asked me why I chose the academy as the possible site for my school and company, I answered, "Because it is on sacred ground."

But all the land here is sacred ground. Sacred to the Indians, sacred even before the Indians lived here. What strange animals lived here, what strange people and plants. All rests on holy ground. Ground that is dedicated to life—to the wonder of life.

One by one the sisters come to greet me, dressed formally in the black and white habits you so rarely see now. Sister Julie said to me that my dance does what they hope to achieve in their Mass, a communication in unity of the spirit of man. The sisters said they thought of me as a mystic. But I do not think of myself that way at all.

With my Presbyterian upbringing it was such a relief to learn that "sin," in archery, means "missing the mark." The Bible is filled with

273

wonderful stories, particularly the Old Testament. I'd like to be known as a storyteller. I have a holy attitude toward books. If I was stranded on a desert island I'd only need two, the dictionary and the Bible. Words are magical and beautiful. They have opened up new worlds to me. I'm a very strange reader; I like espionage. Nothing lets me think more clearly through a problem than reading and alternating between two mysteries at the same time. Odd, but it works.

From my days in the *Follies* it has been my practice most evenings to gather some of my favorite books around me in bed, and take excerpts from them in green stenography notebooks. Recently, after a few scrawls, I began to grow very restless. I was beginning my new work, *Maple Leaf Rag*. As much as I resisted it my mind went back to the days when I worked with Louis Horst in the 1930s. I don't know where we were, probably in one of those unfriendly cold and drafty studios that overlooked Central Park. I dragged myself to the window and put my head in my hands, a sure sign to long-suffering Louis that his Mirthless Martha was on the road to a major black Irish depression. But I didn't want one just yet. And so I looked up at Louis and pleaded, "Oh, Louis. Play me the 'Maple Leaf Rag.'" And he did. It worked as it had before; it released me for a little time from the fear I had.

Maple Leaf Rag is a fairly joyous dance. It's not the music I would have chosen fifty years ago. In a way, it is another railroad, like the one that brought me from the East to the West many years ago. I remember being in the back of that train, in the caboose, seeing the land we had traversed. It always meant something to me. You're going on. Maybe it is a strange road without houses. But it is the impulse of the engine that drives you and you arrive at your destination in spite of the great land which you had inherited. That, to me, is life. Life is not giving up, but moving on.

The pauses between rehearsals in a theatre are the most agonizing. All you can think of is where you failed.

.   .   .

Now it is October 1990. I sit in a very dark dressing room at the City Center Theatre, facing another fear, one I cannot call upon my years of training to meet. *Maple Leaf Rag* has had a world premiere of great success, but it means little to me, even though I had gone onstage to take the final curtain call. For now I am facing the most depressing time for anyone in the theatre, the weeks that follow a season. You are sure nothing will ever happen, good or bad. It is the end. It does not help that we leave for Tokyo in two weeks to begin our Asian tour.

Finally, the theatre is empty and I walk past the only light left in any theatre when everything is closed and everyone is gone. It is a single glaring light bulb resting on top of a long bare black metal pole placed on midstage. It is called the ghost light, a symbol of all of the lives and legends that are still in this theatre, and that in some form go on.

I'm asked so often at ninety-six whether I believe in life after death. I do believe in the sanctity of life, the continuity of life and of energy. I know the anonymity of death has no appeal for me. It is the now that I must face and want to face.

I have a new ballet to do for the Spanish government, and I have been brooding about pointing it toward the transmigration of the goddess figure, from India to Babylon, Sumer, Egypt, Greece, Rome, Spain (with its Dama del Elche), and the American Southwest. And I am sure it will be a terror and a joy, and I will regret starting it a thousand times, and think it will be my swan song, and my career will end like this, and I will feel that I have failed a hundred times, and try to dodge those inevitable footsteps behind me. But what is there for me but to go on? That is life for me. My life.

How does it all begin? I suppose it never begins. It just continues.

And one . . .

With gratitude to these dear friends and colleagues: Aboudi, Russ Alley, Takako Asakawa, Mark Bahti, Polly Bergen, Telsa Bernstein, Stacie Bristow, Sandy Calder, Joseph Campbell, Jacques Cellier, Aaron Copland, Imogen Cunningham, Agnes de Mille, Bethsabée de Rothschild, Doris Duke, Michele Étienne, Betty Ford, Carol Fried, Milton Goldman, Ann Gray, Diane Gray, Neel Halpern, Linda Hodes, Louis Horst, Kennan Hourwich, Bianca Jagger, James Johnson, Angela Kapp, Donna Karan, Tom Kerrigan, Yuriko Kimura, Calvin Klein, Deborah Kramm, Pearl Lang, Richard Lawson, Peggy Lyman, Madonna, Dr. Allen Mead, Ted Michaelsen, Barbara Morgan, Peter Morrison, Dr. Jeffrey Nakamura, Isamu Noguchi, Rudolf Nureyev, Nancy Oakes, Gregory and Veronique Peck, Alexander Racolin, Todd Randall, Terry Rhein, Jerome Robbins, Jean Rosenthal, Kevin Rover, Carroll Russell, Peggy Shields, Gertrude Shurr, Dr. Irwin and Lucia Smigel, Ruth St. Denis, Peter Stern, Walter Terry, Kathleen Turner, Russ Vogler, Linda Wachner, Lila Acheson Wallace, Gay Wray, Dr. Rachel Yocom.

INDEX OF PHOTOGRAPHY